GETTING
CUSTOMERS

Easier, faster and for **less money**
than you ever thought possible

JAMES SINCLAIR

MEREO

Mereo Books

1A The Wool Market Dyer Street Cirencester Gloucestershire GL7 2PR
An imprint of Memoirs Book Ltd. www.mereobooks.com

GETTING CUSTOMERS: 978-1-86151-944-3

First published in Great Britain in 2019
by Mereo Books, an imprint of Memoirs Books Ltd.

The address for Memoirs Books Ltd. can be
found at www.memoirspublishing.com

Memoirs Books Ltd. Reg. No. 7834348

Typeset in 11/15pt Century Schoolbook
by Wiltshire Associates Ltd.
Printed and bound in Great Britain

CONTENTS

CHAPTER 7
Writing to get customers

CHAPTER 8
Final thoughts

For Harvey, my boy

You'll be our legacy, the next generation – live life to the full.

Be kind, and grab life as you wish to enjoy it.

Remember, money recycles and you can get as much as you want or need. Our time is far more precious; use it wisely.

Surround yourself with good and amazing people. They'll be infectious to you as you will to them.

At just two years old, you fill our hearts with joy and laughter. I do hope there'll be proper books around when you join the age of "grumpy grown up".

All our love
Mummy and Daddy.

Acknowledgements

We all need loyalty and support in our life of entrepreneurship. Many have helped me and I have mentioned them in my other books.

Peter Quinn and Alex Demetriou – you've been my guardian angels. Thank you. I love you to the moon and back.

To Mark Creaser: you taught me more about marketing than anyone else I know, and there's a good chunk of this book that has fed my brain with your wit and knowledge. Thank you.

INTRODUCTION

Finding, getting and keeping customers is the most significant and important skill set of a successful start-up entrepreneur. And it's equally vital to the established business too.

Customers are the life blood of any business. That's so obvious it's hardly worth stating, yet so many business people are useless at actually getting them.

Looking at the more established businesses – if that's you – in my experience, the longer a business trundles along, the lazier it becomes at getting more customers. They spend too much time proudly telling everyone about their past successes and reminding everyone that they have been around since the year dot rather than actually working at getting more customers, or keeping them.

Worse than that, when it comes to getting their existing customers to do more with them, they fumble around like toddlers learning to walk. This is plain sad, because existing customers are the low-hanging fruit, the easy pickings. When it comes to marketing to existing customers, you can run before you can walk, because there are quick wins just waiting for you. This group of customers is the stream of gold that most businesses don't tap into.

If you're a start-up, getting customers should trump all other tasks. After all, *no customers, no business!*

If you want to find out what marketing actually works, what marketing actually gets customers, then this is the book for you. In this book, getting customers will come first.

This is the view of a bloke who has no formal marketing qualifications. This is the view of a bloke who has built a multi-million-pound business from scratch, starting in his teens. This is the view of a bloke who has actually done it, gone out there and won customers from nothing, with no money to invest – and in later years with some money, which brings its own challenges.

Professional marketing types often fail to practise what this book teaches. I'm going to show you why a guerrilla warfare approach is better than a concerted mass attack. Am I tickling your taste buds yet? If so, read on.

In this book I will set out to show the frustrated business owner who's trying to make ends meet, signing the cheques and knowing every penny counts, how to get customers.

If your organisation values design first and you work in a shiny office building made of glass with a reception area the size of a tennis court, then I hope to challenge the brand marketing based approach and instead show you methods that will actually get you the customers you want – NOW. It's for you guys and gals too. We're fighting the same war – it's just that the methods in this book may be different from those you are used to.

Here's some great news. You won't need a marketing budget the size of Donald Trump's tax bill to implement the methods I'm going to tell you about . You will just need the ability to put ideas into action. Business people so often fail to do that. You don't have to be a quantum physicist to realise that making your plans actually HAPPEN will give you a huge advantage over those who just talk about it.

This book is not for someone who's trying to build the new sexy brand of the day, or make a comical video that wins eyeballs for a brand's look and feel to 'create awareness'. I'll say it again – this is the book to **get customers**, because where do we want them and when do we want them? **HERE, and NOW!**

I'm going to reassure the business owner who wants to understand the fundamentals of marketing as a defence against being bamboozled by the self-styled marketing whizzes, people who in many cases waste valuable pounds – YOUR valuable pounds – on pretty ideas that won't do the job well for your business.

This book will show you how to get customers on a shoestring (hurrah!) It will be simple to read (hurrah!) It will make you money (hurrah!) and it will not muddy the waters with trendy jargon. Any technical or industry terminology will be simplified and explained.

I will show you how to get customers by spending money too, but I'll make it super affordable and show you how to achieve a great ROI (return on investment).

So grab a comfy chair, strap yourself in, pour yourself a cuppa and let's get some CUSTOMERS.

Hang on, who is this over-confident, under-qualified marketing bigmouth?

I'm James Sinclair. I sometimes struggle to pinpoint exactly what I am, because I'm a bit of a chameleon. In my teens I was a children's entertainer, which is how it all started. Now I own and run a successful family entertainment and leisure business. We're in the business of building brands that families love-it's my life work. I love property investment too, this helps me in my quest for leverage. As our property interests rise in value, we use that money to grow our physical businesses.

As an entertainer and my love of the stage I've also taken this skill to the business speaking sector, helping entrepreneurs learn from my trials and tribulations, so they too can soar to success.

So I guess I'm a motivational speaker, the author of two previous business books, a business advisor and a business YouTuber. I'm also CEO of the Partyman Group of Companies and Twizzle Tops Day Nurseries, employing 450 staff and turning over millions of pounds. But in my heart, I'm just an entertainer who loves being on stage – that's how it all started, because I made my first bucks, the cash I needed to start building a business, by clowning at kids' parties.

Our core business is a bricks and mortar chain of family entertainment centres called Partyman, with family fun parks and day nurseries part of my business portfolio too. We also make teddy bears - a lot of them. Our company Teddy Tastic, the Make a Bear Company, has made and sold over one million teddy bears. I'd love to dwell on our property portfolio and why I think that property is a smart move for entrepreneurs and companies to divest some time and energy, but that story is for another book.

When I'm asked what I do, I mention just one or two of the things I get up to, because there's just never enough time to go through them all. But all of them need customers, and as we flick through the pages of this book together, you'll get to know exactly what we do in these businesses to get customers – real examples, put to work and used. Tried and tested. We've bought the T-shirt too.

Essentially, what I do is to help my companies get customers and then work out how to use these customers to grow the business. Together we'll be looking closely at your marketing using bang up-to-date methods and old-fashioned techniques which right now seem innovative because they've been forgotten, but in my book are huge opportunities to compete with the big boys, cheaply.

I started flirting with business when I was at school, and quickly fell in love with it. I've been in love with it ever since. My family and friends would call me a workaholic. Can you really be called a workaholic if you spend your life doing the thing you love most? But it's not work I love – it's success.

At the time of writing, I've been getting customers for my businesses for 18 of my 34 years. I spend my time working hard to build our brands, always following that core vision to create and build brands that families LOVE. We are always looking to innovate and improve, always looking to make sure people know about us and what we do.

As a personal mission, I've been helping entrepreneurs soar to success so that they too can change their little corner of the world. I have loved seeing people's lives, and businesses, change after they come to my seminars, or see me speak at conferences or watch my videos.

Today my businesses welcome over a million customers every year. We still start new businesses from scratch, constantly winning new customers with different needs and desires.

From a marketing point of view, I've always nestled myself close to the customer-getting side of the business, leaving operations, admin, accounts, HR and all the other departments to skilled people for whom these are their core strengths. I still think it's the number one most important skill of entrepreneurship. If you can get customers, and fast, you'll solve most of your business's problems.

Many firms spend 80% of their time on operations and only 20% on building the business. it should be the other way round. Doing it my way, I dedicate most of my energies to getting customers to get to where we're going, leaving the great team I've built around me to make sure the operation is delivering for the customers in the operation of the business.

As my career has rocketed along, I have developed a real bug for helping other business owners and speaking at business events about what I've learned. I speak at conferences all over the world. I spend a big chunk of my time making video content on entrepreneurship and marketing and I've made daily documentaries and video blogs on YouTube and all the other major platforms, doing all I can to help. (search James Sinclair on YouTube)

With all that self-indulgence out the way – let's make some magic happen. Let's go!

Chapter 1
Basic business

Hello, getting customers supremo in the making! My hope is that after reading this book you'll have the confidence, tools and knowledge to achieve significant success in getting customers for your business. My other books are well worth a read too, but you can also listen to my podcasts or watch my videos on YouTube, where you'll find a ton of my content, all free to consume.

You see, knowing some little nuggets about broader business issues is essential to leverage what marketing you can do, so that when you do have a little cash to invest, you can turn it into a lot more.

Marketeers are the fortune makers. Knowing about business lets you keep that fortune.

There's a reason you know who Steve Jobs was, who Elon Musk and Sir Richard Branson are: they're marketeers with business nous. You need both sets of knowledge, marketing and running a business, to win. In the getting of customers, certainly the basics of business will be a huge help.

Let me enlighten you with three key important points which will make you appreciate what marketing can *really* do, should your business start to rocket as I hope it will.

Here they are:

Average Customer Value (ACV)

One of the most important things you need to know in business and in your marketing plan – *What is your Average Customer Value? (ACV)* It's dead simple to work out: turnover divided by number of customers. The tracking of it varies from business to business, but your ACV must be consistent and rise year on year. In our companies we have an ACV target. The higher your ACV, the more exciting and rewarding your marketing can get.

I've worked with so many companies who don't even know their ACV. Until you know it, you can't improve it.

While this book is about getting customers, you also have to understand the harsh reality that an increase in ACV is far more profitable than getting a new customer. You see, once they're a customer you're not paying to acquire them, so getting them to spend more or making a plan for their spend to increase is the smartest thing to do.

TOP TIP: ACV needs to be part of your culture for it to work. This means you have to share it with the team so they understand it and can work to improve it.

Average Transactional Value (ATV)

ATV is a close cousin to ACV. We must know how often, on average, customers will transact with us. If your ACV is low and your ATV is low too, it'll always be a hard slog – not impossible but hard work.

Some companies have very high ACV but low ATV – selling cars

2

would be a good example of this, because each customer may only buy a car once every four years. So would selling houses, as an estate agent.

Thinking about ACV and ATV helps you to understand which customers you should be going after.

Average Lifetime Value (ALV)

Knowing the lifetime value of our customers helps us plan how we can literally buy customers with offers and freebies, all in the knowledge that what we've done is kick the can down the road to collect our profit at a later date. Knowing how much a customer is worth over their lifetime is just brilliant when it comes to planning marketing spend for getting customers.

Lastly, never forget this: in business, MARGIN is your superpower.

Margin is, in my view, crucial for long-term success. It allows the owner to properly invest, innovate and really look after customers to turn them into raving fans. Decent margin will allow businesses to thrive rather than just survive, like most, or as in even more cases, die.

To operate as most businesses do, on what I call a 'sliver of margin', to win, you'll be shoehorned into achieving giant scale to make any decent profits. Pick up any business newspaper and you'll see some giant corporation announce that it has made pre-tax profits of say £23 million. Wow! Until you read that this was on sales of £900 million. The point is that giant turnover can produce what looks like big profit, but isn't. I've operated businesses with brilliant margin and lots of others with just a sliver of margin. Every time I have had more fun with the large margin businesses, because the customers are more profitable and the businesses are always stronger. Plus, with decent margin the marketing effort is ten times better.

I think of the amazing loyalty of customers to companies like Disney and Apple – why? Because their margin is so much greater that they can invest to stay the best, simply because their margin allows them to do this.

Product first. Marketing second.

If you're marketing a dead duck, it will always be a dead duck. Your products or services have to be good, so that your marketing efforts get word of mouth superpower as they work alongside them.

Marketing must come after product. If you've got good product, make sure you market it. We MUST market our products and services, even when they are so unbelievably good that we feel we don't need to.

I believe you have to be working on your business to a point. Smart entrepreneurs put mechanisms in place that enable them to dive back in and make sure the product is always as good as their marketing claims. Nothing's worse than telling the world your product is the best in the market and then discovering that whoops, not any more it isn't.

Be 80% on your business and 20% in it.

In any business you need a set of people running a system you've created with them, not a system they have created without your involvement.

Let me give you an example. Over the last six months I have been putting some ambitious plans together for Marsh Farm, our animal adventure park. We want to turn the place into a zoo and double our visitor numbers – it's innovation of our product to achieve our goals. I need a cracking year with strong numbers and a credible plan to present to the bank and planners to let me do it. It's product before marketing planning.

We come back to two things to keep you ahead, INNOVATION and MARKETING, and in this case something NEW to market – which is always lazy marketing, but it works. People love NEW. We must never forget that having something new to say with innovative marketing is a power tool for the marketeer. Forget to keep on it, and staleness can creep up on you.

Worse still, if you're doing well and cash is flowing in like a river, be aware that your competitors will be catching you up. You can ride that river for a while and live on your past success, but only for so long.

TOP TIP: Innovate – or evaporate

As Sony did, before Apple jumped on them in tech.
As Tesla has done to cars with their competitors desperately trying to innovate and catch up.

When it comes to marketing, the general gist is that there are 4 camps of business owner:

1. 'My reputation and product are so good I don't need to market – my product/service does it for me.'
2. 'I spend more time on marketing and when I have time, I dive into operations to make sure we're doing what we should.
3. 'I spend all my time on operations, and IF I have time I do some marketing.'
4. 'My product or service is good, but no one knows about me.'

Why you MUST market

Before we go further, read the next statement – many times!

'The business owner should be a marketeer above all other skills. They will have a team in place to make sure product is consistent, to give them the will to market with more confidence.'

Some people believe that a great product markets itself, and to an extent I agree. A great product will slowly over time get you a degree of custom, but it will be a constant trickle rather than a flood. Our job is to create the flood!

'Build it great and they will come' is a big lie. Build it great and do a great job of marketing it – THEN they'll come.

We all know that word of mouth is the greatest form of marketing - it's just slow. Really good marketing ignites the flame that makes word of mouth so much more powerful. If your product's good and marketing keeps reminding your customers HOW good, then your pounds invested in marketing bring bigger dividends.

If you find you're doing really well with no marketing effort, then my personal opinion is this: you're sleeping on a gold mine. All you have to do is open up that mine and let people discover it.

I was talking to a business friend from sunny Yorkshire the other day. He said in his broad Yorkshire accent, 'We get 400,000 customers a year, and we spend nowt on marketing'. I replied, 'I bet if you spent some money on marketing you'd have 500,000 customers a year'. I could see the cogs going round as he thought about that. The reason he does well – and the reason he can do even better – is that his product is so good.

We MUST market, regardless of how we feel it's all going. The simple truth is this: a great product needs to be pushed to front of mind. The dangerous part of a good thing is that someone else will always want to take it over. In time, they'll succeed, if you let them. They'll take your customers away with good product and marketing. If you're really unlucky, they'll add some innovation too – then you'll need to start again, and it will take a lot more effort.

Of course, you also need to make sure your product or service STAYS great, because what's great today may be old hat tomorrow, especially in technology and IT. Don't let someone develop something better behind your back and steal a lead from you which you may never get back.

I have played the seesaw game with marketing, pulling back the cost and feeling gleefully proud of myself for the improved short-term profits – but then found it was heavy going again as the goodwill wore off.

6

In our first year at Marsh Farm, we spent close to £200,000 on marketing through radio, people, print and Facebook. We cut it down as we believed goodwill would be driving custom, but we were wrong. We found we had to keep the marketing tap running.

I believe in ROI (Return on Investment) marketing, so I want to know I am getting results. The fact is that if you can PROVE that what you are doing is working, your budget can be unlimited, because you know you'll get the investment back, however much it is. But mostly you don't get that certainty – and you do need it, because otherwise you may be risking money you can't afford to lose.

Customer service is king

You don't need the best website, the best shop front or the best location to win. These all help significantly, but a helpful human being with warm customer service skills is far more important, every time.

The ultimate trick is to be consistent – to give the customer certainty. McDonalds haven't got so big through brilliance – they win because they deliver the same 'OK' product every single time, in every single one of their 37,000 restaurants around the world. They never let the food or the service deviate from their own precise standard. It may not be the best food in the world, but it is never bad. It's always good value and you always know what you're going to get and how you're going to get it, whether you're in Putney or Peru. That's what they're brilliant at.

So many businesses fail here. They hopscotch between good, bad, OK and excellent, depending on who's in charge on the day. This is disastrous. If you decide excellence is your aim, then stay excellent – always. If you decide good is a better fit, stay good. Don't try to build a business on a promise you can't deliver. So many companies come up with airy mission statements promising to the most wonderful company you've ever seen. Customers don't believe them – and they're not looking for brilliance anyway. They want what they believe you can deliver.

Now we've got that covered, we can go get customers.

Remember you're the ringleader, not one of the acts

At times I get envious of those who are the number 2, 3 or 4 in a company. Being the ringleader isn't all it's cracked up to be. Sometimes it's better to be the star act in the circus instead. You still get to make a real difference, without having the monumental pressure of knowing that the buck really does stop with you. I have had the sleepless nights, the awful 'How am I going to do this?' moments. I know what it's like to hate being away and to be unable to enjoy a few days off.

I'll tell you what has always got me through – the seriously great band of number 2s, 3s and 4s who have been my lieutenants in running a business that grows every year and has a clear vision of what the end of the journey looks like.

I am not self-made – no one is. I have had help from an amazing team, who've become great friends. My MD, Aaron, who's been working with me since he was 19, has been through good times and bad along the journey as we built my business, The Partyman Company. No company is constantly up – there are too many moving parts and there's a constantly changing environment, always with new storms to face. Our great team has helped me navigate those storms.

I'm labelled self-made because I rolled the dice to start the whole thing. At 16 years old I started building a business. I employed people and invested in property as soon as I could. I've personally guaranteed and borrowed millions and millions of pounds. That's something most people won't do – after all, the odds of success are firmly stacked against you. The truth is, most businesses fail. We put self-made people on pedestals because from a distance they appear to have achieved what most people just cannot do, because they take the risk. As I have come to appreciate, they have different DNA.

Was I right to do what I did? Who knows? Is it worth the unrelenting challenge? I'm not so sure, but I am where I am, and I won't be changing any day soon.

Close family and friends can't work out why I keep going, when I could lead the life of Riley just by living on my investments and enjoying my speaking career. The reason is, I have entrepreneurial DNA. I am a builder of things, and a collector. I want to build something for my senior team to enjoy and reward from. I like to create, and more than that, I have a relentless long-term view mixed with impatient needs. I know that when it comes to building something substantial, the difference between success and failure in business is on a knife's edge. At times it feels like sailing the seven seas in a canoe, over giant waves which are trying to drown you at every chance they get. It's exhilarating and exciting and downright terrifying, all in one go.

Granted, as the years trundle on, success does gets easier and you learn how to navigate the storms and the waves. You get a bigger boat with more crew to help, then a yacht, then a ferry, then a tanker, then a battleship. You get stronger and smarter – and so does your team.

When it comes to assembling your crew, look to harness your weaknesses – I always have. That means I look for great managers, doers and organisers who fit my attitude, but have contrasting skill sets to me so they are great at what I don't do too well.

When assembling your marketing advisors, contractors or team, the method is the same. They must be thinking the way we do, sharing our attitude. Never be blinded by glorious skill sets. Find the marketeer who understands the principles set out in this book, not just the principles of design, look and feel. Remember – we want customers.

KEY POINTS

To summarise this chapter, you need to be the ringleader of the circus. To put it another way, you're like a GP – literally, the General Practitioner - in a medical practice. That means you need to know all the basics when it comes to building your business and your marketing team, so you can put key questions to the specialist medics you assemble who will implement your plans.

Never restrict yourself to being the specialist in one particular area – that way you're just one of the acts. Far better to know a little about a lot than everything about one thing. If you're an expert in finance, you'll need to learn to hand it over to another finance specialist who, unlike you, can focus on it 100 per cent. If production is your thing, again you'll need to delegate to a full-time expert.

Chapter 2

How brands turbo-charge marketing

Luckily for me, when I started out in entrepreneurship I discovered this fellow called Sir Richard Branson, the founder of the Virgin group. I delved into his first book, *Losing My Virginity*, like a child discovering chocolate for the first time. It's a great book, and it really shaped my entrepreneurial ideology and my approach to getting things done, along with the order I would do them in. In many ways, I realised Branson had been a marketeer before he was an entrepreneur. He also showed me that he plays to his strengths and just buys in his weaknesses – that's a smart thing to do.

Personal brand vs. business brand

Branson's book taught me that a personal brand – yourself – is a much lower-hanging fruit to pick than a company brand. He used himself as a personality to get bundles of publicity – cheaply. (Cheap – that's a word entrepreneurs love when they're starting out.) Like him, I've found I have a knack for starting businesses. It's not your lack of resources that stops things happening, it's your lack of resourcefulness.

TOP TIP: Personal brand is easier to leverage for publicity

That book and others introduced me to the entrepreneurs who had been there, done it and got the T-shirt – Richard Branson for Virgin, Walt Disney for Disney, Steve Jobs for Apple and Elon Musk for Tesla, to name just a few. Whilst their company brands may now have overtaken their founders, in terms of value, there's no denying that giving yourself celebrity appeal as a founder opens doors and gets you noticed. Aside from marketing, the opportunities that come your way in the acquisition of business and contracts are eye watering, and eye-opening. I like to think of a personal brand as a small handle that can open big doors.

Whilst my strong belief is that brand-build marketing shouldn't be a paid-for exercise, unless it's done on a huge scale as Coca Cola do, I am wholeheartedly happy for it to be a time investment exercise rather than a money investment – it works.

Why brand = trust

To me brands are all about trust. As a consumer, when I buy a brand I get that warm KLT feeling – Know, Like and Trust, something you'll learn more about in Chapter 4. Trust puts rocket fuel into your marketing spend. Over time your marketing will build you a brand, and so will your business, when you're doing a good job.

Brand removes friction – it oils the cogs of the buying process. To hammer home the point, allow me to share with you a scenario. Say I put on one of my seminars for business owners and spend £5000 on marketing it. Now suppose Richard Branson does the same thing with the same spend, using the same advertising methods. He'll get a bigger response than me, because his brand is bigger than mine. That's what I mean when I say that brands turbo-charge your marketing spend.

The glorious news is you can build your personal brand like the titans I mentioned above, and you can do it more easily than ever before. We now have access to platforms, and we can all compete with the big boys if we invest the time – an hour a day invested in your personal brand over three years will get you where you want to be.

If this interests you and you see it as a little folly, something to wander down a garden path to, then think again – it takes commitment. It's going to be an hour a day, forever.

The 4 Cs that follow will give you an idea if developing a personal brand is right for you.

Charisma/Character

You'll need to be interesting, even slightly unusual, to grab attention. You can't be boring if you want to win on content marketing/personal brand building. This could even mean you attract or repel viewers – the best go for pistachio ice cream rather than vanilla, meaning the people who like you REALLY like you. Pistachio ice cream isn't for everyone, and you don't have to be either.

A funny thing I've learnt is that the more unusual you are, the more people change and start to like you – over time.

Comfort

You'll need to be comfortable with being public, be comfortable with keyboard warriors and lose no sleep. You need to be the best version of your character that makes you comfortable.

Be comfortable with the personal attacks.

Be comfortable being known.

A good friend said to me that his greatest fear for his children was that they would become famous and miss out on all the simple things in life. Managing fame, even among just a few, takes a level of comfort. You'll have to get comfortable feeling uncomfortable in the world of personal brand.

Content

Next is the actual content. You'll need to deliver this with expertise and authority, to know your onions on your subject and deliver it with passion.

I like to give credit and reference other people's content if I think my audience will value it, better this than take it off as your own.

Here's a couple of things NOT to worry about:

1. Don't always try to create new messages.

I learnt this lesson within a few months of getting into content marketing. It's very rare that you'll continue to have the same viewer or follower on repeat. Keep in mind that most people will be discovering you for the first time, every time. You may feel like you'll be peddling the same content in different ways, but your viewer may have only just discovered you. For the regular viewer it's reminding them of your core message. We don't change our national anthem every we time we sing it!

This is similar to another common problem when you're on the inside looking out at your business – logo fatigue. Business managers see their logo and corporate colours all day and every day, and after a year or two some thrusting executive who wants to make a mark announces that it's time to throw it out and get a new one. But the average customer has only seen it a few times, and they're just beginning to recognise and accept it as a friend. Change it and you risk throwing away the little bit of recognition and acceptance that you have begun to build up.

2. Don't imagine that telling them everything will kill your leads.

We humans are funny creatures. We worry people will copy our ideas; we worry that if we show them how it's done they'll just do it themselves and not pay us to do it. Cast all that aside, my friends! Firstly, people WILL copy your ideas. Always. Secondly, there are no new ideas, just different ways to present them or a slight polish on what was there before.

14

With the whole do-it-yourself thing, nothing could be further from the truth. If customers know you, know what you know, really well, then they're more prepared to buy from you.

3. Be consistent.

Last but not least is consistency. Your content must be as consistent as a TV station. It should not be sporadic, but timed and regular. Your job is to create habits and followers.

The rule of four to create a habit is important. If people watch four videos, or read four articles, then they're well on the way to becoming faithful fans.

A decade ago you needed to have access to TV, newspapers, radio, films and billboards to reach an audience and build personal and company brands – all very expensive and aimed at mass audiences, and extremely competitive even if you had the willpower to do it. Now we've got the internet and the birth of platforms which reach more people than the old conventional media ever could. TV has lost more eyeballs to YouTube than all its competitors combined. Linked In, Facebook, Twitter, YouTube and Instagram are all there for us to use.

The good news – and the bad news – is that everyone and their granny is trying to have a go. But most of them can't be bothered to see it through, and this is where you'll win.

My promise to you is this: if you're good on camera, or at writing articles, or making podcasts, and if you stay constant on content, the payback will be huge.

Be famous to a few

Personal brand creation grows much faster in a niche market, so you should start by becoming famous to a few – leave the masses till later.

This is a much easier task, and will pay dividends to you much sooner. Depth with followers, not superficial awareness among the many, is the way to go. A thousand followers who really want to know you is better than 100,000 who've just about heard your name.

In every industry there are famous leaders who are household names to everyone in that industry, yet almost unknown outside it. For fishing it'll be the go-to fishing expert, the one who catches all the big fish and endorses all the tackle. For the wine industry it will be the prize-winning, innovative winemaker who writes a column in a trade magazine. For IT, it'll be the CEO of the hottest new software company on the block. I will always write an article in the trade press or speak at conferences for the industries we operate in. When people know you, you pull opportunities towards you rather than constantly pushing for them.

TOP TIP: There's riches in niches! Find a niche and dominate it.

Building your personal brand is easy if you have the mentality that you're willing to show up to the opening of a packet of crisps. I did that, every time we started a new business. If the village fete was on, I'd do a magic show and talk about our parties and play centre at the end. When I launched our seminar training business, I'd speak at events with five people; to leverage my time, we'd record that seminar, then get the recording out as video content.

When I started out doing children's entertainment, I did free shows for schools. The personal brand-building task has been of huge importance. I'm a little busier now because of my time value, but still to this day, I see personal PR activities as gold dust for my business.

I'll speak on radio stations which have one listener if I think it will open the door to something. I make YouTube videos by the truckload, and speak or perform wherever there is an audience. I make sure I write articles for local rags and distribute them on my social platforms.

16

I constantly try to leverage my time. I record everything and try to repurpose content to get more eyeballs on it.

The company brand

As part of your marketing you will build your company brand, but as a by-product only. This should never be the primary focus. Getting customers should be your primary focus.

Having a well-known company brand is valuable for sure, but the guerrilla marketeer – that's you – sees building a company brand as a 'sawdust' product. What's a sawdust product? It's when you get a piece of wood and make what the customer wants to buy from it, maybe a piece of furniture. At the end of it, you'll have produced tons of sawdust at no cost. That sawdust has a value, so you can sell it. The sawdust is a by-product – it just happens as a result of your primary focus, in this case making chairs. To me, brand marketing is a sideshow, never the main act.

It's worth hammering home that...

Company brand value best happens organically over time. It's worth protecting and valuing, but only as a by-product. Getting customers is your main task.

Why you need to run four companies in one.

I've been teaching this theory, which I practise of course, at all my seminars for the last few years. I love studying what successful people do and noting what I've done in my career that really worked, then teaching it in a way that's so obvious a kid can get it. This is my view, and I'm pretty sure applying to your business will be a great move.

Most successful people in business set their stall using this methodology. Few do it by planned process. They don't really know they've done it till it's pointed out. After reading this chapter you can do it by planned process yourself.

Here are the four companies I am constantly running:

1. The company we are today.

2. The company we want to be.

3. A media company.

4. A property/investment company.

In effect you're running a media company and an operating company in unison to win. *Hang on, how does that work?* Fear not, enlightenment is coming. The media company floods the operating company with warm leads and customers, like Beyoncé or Lady Gaga bombarding people to buy tickets for their shows or their downloads on iTunes. Celebrities are media companies, providing easy income to operating companies.

Disney was, and obviously still is, a media company that now follows this theory, as I see it – by progression, rather than design. They make films that are loved by billions of people, and it all started with the teenage Walt's passion for illustration. By the time he was 27 he had invented Mickey Mouse. So it has made total sense for them to become an operating company.

If you think about it; Disney makes tons of media, TV shows, films, radio and songs, which in turn have created merchandise in the form of toys, hotels, theme park tickets and cruise ships. These are traditional operating companies, but because of their media they charge more, make more, and get customers far more easily.

The opportunity for the smart marketing-oriented entrepreneur to do the same is now easy to appreciate. As I keep saying, the platforms are so accessible and they're crying for more content.

So let's recap: Our media company, which I call company 3, will push clients, via its media efforts, into companies 1 and 2 – our operating companies. The profits from companies 1 and 2 should be pumped into company 4 (the property investment company). This should act as a pension pot and innovation fund for when the business needs money to innovate again, so it can get more customers.

It's inevitable that at some stage your business will become stale and you'll need to go again with a serious amount of innovation, and this will need cash. Lack of innovation means you rely increasingly on history to stay in business. All companies, at some time in their lives, will have wobbles, because the competition always out-innovates you. To give an example, at the time of writing, retail is going through a huge innovation process, because customers are migrating to on-line and experience-based shopping. Retailers have a choice – innovate or evaporate. Blockbuster took too long to innovate, so Netflix took over. Sometimes funding the catch up is difficult – but that's why you have company 4, to provide funding when you need it.

Trouble is, when problems arise, trying to win is tough. With investments (company 4) you can leverage funding to re-innovate your business and get more customers. Company 4 is iron-clad security that doesn't make fast money. The good news is that banks and investors see investment companies as safe, so they are more willing to lend to them.

So what's the difference between companies 1 and 2 - they're both operating companies?

The above query may have flown through your head, with good reason. The difference is in the title.

Company 1 – the company you are today – is not there yet. It's still climbing the slippery slope. It's got to win market share. You can't have the perfect team yet, or get the prices you really want. You'll make decisions to grab turnover. You'll make decisions that'll keep you surviving.

This company has an owner that wears many hats. They're the head of marketing, sales, operations, HR et al. This is not the way you want your company to be.

The trick is to know when your business will finish – when it will be all you want it to be – and what it will look like at the finish. This is so you make better decisions in company 1 for when you've achieved company 2.

My business started as a family entertainment company. We knew that eventually we wanted to open visitor attractions and build brands that families would love. I felt that this company gave us the best footing to get the experience to be the business we wanted to eventually be – company 2.

Company 2 is the company you *really* want to be. It's what the best version of your company looks like.

Armed with a target date for when this will happen, and a detailed document outlining what the company will actually look like, you'll be on course to build company 2.

The reason I'm talking about a detailed document – a business plan – is because that will provide a clear vision of what company 2 will look like. It holds you to account for what you say you will do.

To kick you off with understanding YOUR company 2, here are the key points I would cover.

–   What does your ideal management team look like?
–   What's your ideal culture like? (Every business has a culture, but very often it's not the right one.)
–   What's your customer avatar? (more on this later)
–   What's your profit and revenue?
–   From where will you be operating?
–   Will you still be needed in the business, day to day? If you will, then you haven't got there yet. I'm not joking. When the business is mature, when building it has finished, you're the owner, the

founder, the person who made it all happen. You are not an operative. In short, you are no longer needed, at least not day to day. Great - you can get on and build another company!

Now we know all we need to know on the business front, let's get some customers.

Chapter 3
Knowing your customer

Customer avatars - who are they?

We must make sure we understand who our customer is now and who the ideal customer is, because knowing who we want to target as customers, who they are and where they are, is the single biggest way to improve our marketing. By customer avatar, I mean the figure who stands for the ideal target customer. Knowing who this person is will bring a big improvement to your marketing efforts.

Most people have an idea of the ideal customer they are after, but it's only an idea. In most cases they settle for the customer that just gets them by, their 'most' customer, the one they actually get most of the time. I like to have a 'most' customer and an 'ideal' customer. Saying, for example, you're marketing to men in their 40s who have a job is a poor description of a customer avatar. This guy is probably just your 'most' customer.

We want to know both our most customer and our ideal customer better: what they earn, where they live, how often they spend, what's their disposable income, what do they see as essential and non-essential spend, who do they see as your competitors, how they feel about your product or service, what their pain points in life are.

For my leisure business, which targets families, I know that for my 'most' customer, disposable income is tight. In fact, I know that a typical family in the UK has about £150 spare money left over per month after the money that's committed monthly to mortgage or rent, household bills, cars etc. I also know that my competition is competing for that same £150.

This knowledge gives me power. Knowing your customer, which, let me remind you, is not YOU, is a superpower. You're probably your own ideal customer, not your 'most' customer.

Knowing that my customer has only £150 a month to spend, I know I'm going to have to help them to pay for what they want from us. For example our annual membership costs £65. For a family of three that's £195 – already that's more than they can afford. So we have a scheme that spreads the cost over a year, based on paying £5 a month. This doesn't just make it affordable, it has another advantage – it encourages them to come back through the year and spreads the business into the winter months.

At this juncture it's worth creating a system and process to remind yourself of this fact. It's human to forget and like most, you will forget – I do.

I have always tried to create a democratic management team around me so that my senior team can tell me what they think. This sounding board and culture of open debate should help in keeping it real when it comes to understanding who your customer is. Lyssa, who works closely with me in our senior team, keeps a picture of our customers on her desk. It's a good way of reminding us who we really need to reach.

It's downright foolish to design marketing around who you think your customer is. Most people do not have the income streams of decision

23

makers and business owners. It's folly to think that just because you and your circle of friends like something, your customer likes it too.

Let's take a moment to look at the difference between the 'ideal' customer and the 'most' customer for my childcare business, if I was setting up from scratch.

The MOST customer:
- Has to pay for childcare so they can work.
- Low disposable income remains after all costs are paid each month.
- Government funding is essential to help towards the cost.
- Wants a close, easy location.
- Must have confidence in the team that delivers the childcare – they want to know that what we do is right for their child.
- Finds price increases hard, as they eat into what little income the family has.
- The cost means sacrifices will be made elsewhere on family expenditure – holidays and days out, for example.
- When childcare is no longer needed, the cost savings are really noticeable.

The IDEAL customer:
- Sees childcare as an investment in their children, so they can work if they choose to or see their children develop.
- Needs our service, loves our setting and, chooses our business.
- Is happy to pay our higher fees because we are outstanding.
- Loves our culture and ethos.
- Is not concerned about, or doesn't notice, an annual price increase.

- The cost does not impact family income enough to force a choice between one thing and another.
- When the children leave it's sad, but the cost saving is not significant.

Most companies live in the 'most' camp, by definition... and that's the reason why eventually, most companies go bust. If you're lucky enough to be able to build a business around the ideal customer, you'll be around for much longer. If you're getting the ideal customer, that usually means you're delivering an experience-based business. That means you'll probably be smaller, but you'll be stronger, and although you may repel the 'most' people you will attract your ideal avatar.

I'm so passionate about this ideal that I wrote a book about it – check it out, it's called *The Experience Business.*

It's quite something to work out who your ideal customer is. It makes you better on all fronts. You get better at delivery and better at looking after customers, and you attract better staff too.

For my business seminar company we have also identified our ideal customer:

- Must employ people.
- A good business owner looking to be great, not someone who needs rescuing.
- Revenues of at least £250,000.
- Ambitious to grow.
- We can easily see how to help them.
- We enjoy working with them.
- They *smell* successful.
- No start-ups.

These points, plus a few more, allow us to really direct our efforts to get customers.

The great news is that 1000 'ideal' customers can trump 10,000 'most' customers.

The tree needs to be fed before you can pick the fruit.

At seminars I like to draw this tree to explain most and ideal customers. I do love a doodle and an explanation of it to explain my point.

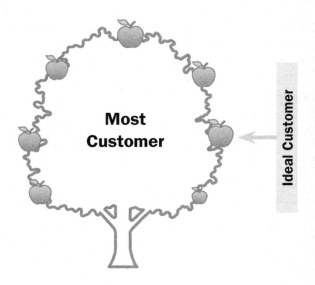

Google's most customers don't pay them anything – Google give the gift of search for free. They also give Google maps for free – they give many things for free. These free items are for their most customers. It's their tree that makes their ideal customers grow – their fruit.

We now buy from Google, as do so many companies,. After a time we became their fruit giving them easy pickings. We buy email servers from them, storage and pay-per-click to get customers. My business does this because they have a strong tree.

The thing to remember is that the last thing to grow on a tree, is the fruit.

I love this model. In my seminar business most of my customers are viewers of my content. This allows me to get my consultancy clients easily.

Our leisure business gets members, ideal customers, and day nursery clients are an even more ideal customer, all on the strength of our most customer.

So many companies just have either ideal or most customers. The smart ones have both.

TOP TIP: Customer avatars - you need to know your MOST customer and your IDEAL customer. This improves the way you market, because, you now know your target market.

LAW 1
Market, Message, Media - in that order

When it comes to marketing, there are two laws I follow in my pursuit of getting customers. Law 1 is Market, Message and Media. Law 2 will follow.

Knowing our customer avatar allows us to think smartly about our market, which should always be the primary thought in marketing and creating a marketing project. Who's our market? What's the solution my product or service delivers, or more to the point solves? That is where I start and finish where prospects are concerned.

Most people think about media first. They say to themselves, or their team – let's put something on YouTube, or in the press, or on radio. Now let's decide what to say – the message. Only last do they ask themselves about the market they're trying to reach. This is completely the wrong way round. Always you need to start with the person you're trying to reach – your customer avatar, then decide on the right message, and finally the most appropriate media to get that message across to your target.

This is getting to be a more common mistake, as media are cheap (and in many cases free). With free accessible media, business owners post away on the various platforms with no thought as to who their market is, where they are and what message will make them take action to benefit the business.

Imagine if you'd started marketing campaigns by choosing media 30 years ago. Of course that never happened, because just making a TV ad would have cost a small fortune, let alone buying the airtime. To invest in a filmed commercial would have been a board decision. A plan of why and how the campaign would work would have been presented. Now you can just write a message on a smartphone and you're away, without a single careful thought.

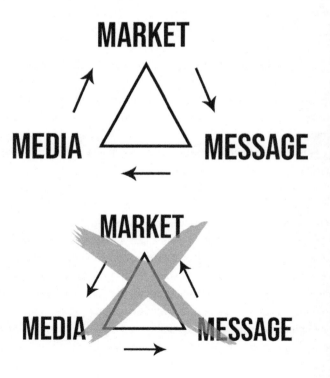

In most cases business owners think 'we must do some marketing, I'll post something on Facebook, send a tweet, send an email'. What a stupid waste of time that is in the getting of customers. It is poor awareness marketing at best and at worse can blow your chance of getting customers.

When it comes to marketing, you should ask yourself how you can get a reaction and action from your potential customers (your market). You should not feel happy that you've done enough just by posting your company logo and services every now and then.

The media you use to post or distribute your marketing message should be a decision born out of getting your market and message correct. The danger is that because you consume social media stuff so readily everywhere, you copy other poor marketing, and there's a good chance they've got it wrong.

First identify your market, then the message you want to deliver, what you want to sell to turn into pounds. What's the pain you solve for your customers? What do they want from you more than anything else? Try with all your might NOT to sell features in your message – in fact you shouldn't even be selling benefits. You need to sell the SOLUTION.

Example: a sleeping bag. Feature: an extra layer of insulation. Benefit: It will keep you warmer on a cold night. Solution: You'll get a good night's sleep and wake up ready for a great day's camping.

What about a smartphone? Feature: 4G ready. Benefit: You can use it to surf the internet. Solution: You can work anywhere in the world!

To put it another way, it's the WOW that sells, not the HOW.

You need a really powerful message that will cause a reaction. I make sure my message solves the problem – I don't fiddle with the details.

The message should drive people to make decisions and give them a strong desire to buy.

Armed with a knowledge of your market and your killer message, then it's time to think what media you should use – which media have the highest chance of getting eyeballs for your carefully crafted message.

Choosing your media

Your media choice is critical. *The response you get is going to be solely down to who reads or sees it,* so you must make sure it's in the right place.

The fact is, some media, and as we know there are lots of them out there, will give far greater returns than others, depending on who your customer is and where they go.

If you want to get investors reading your piece, it's pretty obvious that the *Financial Times* is a better bet than the *Daily Mirror*.

TOP TIP: Remember – for attention grabbing, it's wow not how

In the UK, the biggest selling paid-for newspaper at the time of writing is The *Sun*. Many people dismiss it as tripe, but actually it's a marvel of copywriting (more on that shortly) and a marketing textbook on how to get attention. They win because they grab you in, they WOW you, not how you.

They win hands-down in understanding their market and what the message is, and in this case they ARE the media. They have got this way through raw competition over many years with a product that has to sell every day of the year, every year, to survive, against equally fierce competitors. Survival of the fittest has put *The Sun* where it is, and in this case the fittest is simply the daily newspaper that grabs the most readers. Their advertising customers get this, and because they understand their customers they continue to advertise. The more copies the paper sells, the more success their advertisers have. More sales means more advertisers means staying in business.

The heading is a powerful message that sells the story to you in a matter of a few words, usually no more than four or five. They sell the key point of the story to you before you've bought the paper, or even opened it. For example: 'BUST BRITAIN – 1M JOBS THREATENED' or 'POP STAR SLAYS GRANNY'. The headline is designed to create shock, fear, fascination – and those emotions make you want to find out more. You buy the paper to read the details, and in seconds they have gained another customer – you.

The publishers know their customer avatar, and they know he or she will respond positively to the heading. They know their market. If you think it wouldn't work for you, that's probably because they're not selling to you – they are selling to the millions of people who buy tabloid newspapers.

What's more, that shock headline isn't the only message there to lure you in. Look what else is on the front page – it might be 'Secrets of the X-Factor Winner' or 'Win a Car' or 'How to Dress Like Meghan'. Lots more reasons to buy!

Let's recap. They know their market and they craft a message for it. In this example, they have complete control, because they ARE the media. This all works because they know from hard experience what their customer responds to.

All traditional news outlets now share their stories and their messages on other platforms. They advertise on TV, they get their newspapers onto TV shows and they share stories on social media platforms. This comes second to the message. They think about the customer first and the media last. This is the right way round. This is how you get customers.

Lazy marketing is thinking, 'we must put something out'. Stupid!

LAW 2
AIDA: Attention – Interest – Desire – Action!

The second law to follow in crafting marketing that gets customers is **AIDA**. This juicy little formula literally changed my life when I stumbled across it. I can't quite remember who taught me it, or where I read it, it just works. It gives you a simple little system to plan your marketing message in the right order.

I have spoken to marketeers who have said that not following this four-part rule means all your marketing effort is wasted. I quite agree. If you just adopt two or three of them you won't get half the results, or three-quarters – you'll get no results at all. You MUST have all four. That's because you have to take a 'cold' prospect right through that four-stage process to turn them into a customer.

Think about what happens when you make a purchase. You're never going to buy, say, a new sofa without first noticing that it's for sale (attention), then thinking about it (interest), then deciding you want it (desire), then finally digging out your plastic to buy it (action).

Just as a cub scout remembers his scout promise, marketeers must remember AIDA – and use it in crafting every piece of marketing they do, if they want it to work.

Let's delve in to the nitty gritty, so we can really understand how it works in practice.

Attention

When I make a video, write a sales letter, post something on social media, decide on a book title, design a leaflet, build a website or craft a podcast, I know I have seconds to get people's attention – and so do you, because we're no different.

Attention could quite simply be the most valuable resource in the world right now. All marketing starts with getting attention.

So how do you do it?

By using powerful, startling headings, attention-grabbing images, a 'what's in it for me' video intro – all help to grab attention. I have often said that all marketing comes down to the heading. If the heading doesn't get your customers' attention, they will never bother to find out what comes after it.

They say you should never judge a book by its cover, but where any kind of transaction is concerned, that's exactly what we all do. Getting the right attention means you've got a far higher chance of getting customers.

Interest

Once we have our prospect's **attention**, we have to keep their **interest**. We must not lose these golden seconds.

Great copy keeps you reading a sales letter. A punchy, inspiring video with lots of cuts and brilliant tonality and presentation keeps you watching. People are busy and short of time and interest is quickly lost, so don't be boring. How can you keep their interest?

Stories sell, facts tell. There's a big difference. Telling your kids to do something only works sometimes. Telling them a story has a far better chance of selling them on what you want them to do. So if possible, try and weave stories into your marketing.

Interest simply means we have to keep them engaged. In videos we do this with cuts, music and a strong presenter who combines personality, tonality and body language – it's the same method I use when I am speaking on stage.

Desire

The prospect needs to want what you're selling. So we now need to craft the marketing piece for the shopper to give them a **desire** to buy and become a customer. We need to make them want it, not just think it would be useful one day. Even business buyers are driven in large part by emotion, not logic.

Here are some quick pointers:

- Create a guarantee to reassure the buyer that he/she is not taking a risk.
- Add testimonials, success stories or proof via reviews.
- Don't be too analytical – it's boring and kills desire.

Action

This is the money bit, the bit that's so often forgotten. We need to be as clear as spring water about what **action** we want our prospect to take, and when.

For me to respond I want a deadline, a limited offer and a feeling that this won't be around forever. It also needs to be made real. So many business people get AID right but stop short of AIDA. They don't get the call to action right. People are busy, so we need to make it quick and easy to buy NOW, not some time in the future, if they've decided they like us. Otherwise their interest will fade and they'll forget all about you, and buy later from someone else, or not at all. How many times have you seen an interesting product on sale, thought 'I wouldn't mind some of that' and then been distracted or turned the page and forgotten all about it? Or maybe you remembered a week later, but couldn't remember the name of the company, or where you saw the ad.

TOP TIP for crafting written marketing: 80% heading, 20% content.

Grabbing attention – offline

Approach your marketing as if you're running for local government

When I was 18, I bought a van for our little entertainment company. I covered it in signwriting, including a giant picture of my face grinning like a Cheshire cat, a rubber chicken hanging out the front and flashing lights like a police car lights on top. I know what you're thinking – blimey, that's a bit much! – but for the attention-grabbing marketeer that I am, it still wasn't enough.

Where did I get further inspiration? I was walking somewhere and realized that it was election season, and local candidates were fighting to get elected as our MP. One party had a car with a PA system on top of it, blowing their message out as they drove along: 'VOTE FOR ME'.

I stole the idea and put it on my entertainment van. It really grabbed people's attention. It was unusual to have a PA system on a van and put your message out in this way. People rang me up and booked me and asked me to visit their road.

So there's a lot we can learn about getting customers from watching election campaigns. Like newspapers, the proof that it works, is immediate – the newspaper sells more copies today, the politician gets more votes this week. So look at what they do and how they do it.

First and foremost, they have a date by which they need to win people's votes. This puts a deadline on them and customers, or voters. Powerful stuff. They know their market, they have a message and they use a variety of 'media' – communication channels:

-	Knock on doors and have a chat.
-	Radio station interviews.
-	Posters in supporters' houses.
-	Press articles.
-	Cars touring with PA systems.
-	Visits local businesses to meet owners and colleagues (and get press publicity).
-	Give speeches.
-	Leaflet drops.
-	Canvassers campaigning for them in the street.
-	Letters in the post.

(By the way – notice we haven't even touched the internet yet.)

In other words, they go to the people. Every time I have done this, we have got customers. If cash is tight, then this hard work, low-cost approach will pay dividends.

Frankie, one of our nursery managers, really took this to heart, and it taught me a good lesson. She has made our nursery grow by 100% over the last few years because she knew where her customers hung around and went to talk to them.

Marketing offline to drive online is now very smart, because fewer and fewer marketeers are doing it.

My view, as with investing: *'Observe the masses, then do the opposite'*.

The internet is powerful, and the marketing examples in this book focus on it more than anything else, but nevertheless, the businesses I'm involved in still love sending letters in the post and turning up to where the people are. Offline marketing is still powerful too.

My argument here is that I am simply demonstrating why sending an email or doing a Facebook ad is becoming less and less powerful as more and more people are doing it.

The internet platforms have so many advantages. We can track what a customer does with pixels and cookies (a way of following a browser round the internet), which is hugely valuable. It's just that I like to get people direct to us rather than via some other internet platform.

To recap: *It's smart to drive people to where you want them to go online via your offline marketing efforts.*

How do you make it happen? Simple: you use offline marketing, as above, to grab people's attention, then you use the internet to make the sale happen.

TOP TIP when using this approach: Make sure you turn up on every relevant occasion to give interviews and get yourself some PR.

Chapter 4

What makes people buy

The laws presented in the last chapter, namely Market, Message Media and AIDA, are the foundations of my views on marketing. What puts coal in the getting-customers steam engine is really knowing what makes people buy. It's wise to remember that we too are consumers, so we must try our hardest to remember what makes us take action to do something.

Here are my key points:

KLT: Know, Like and Trust

The easiest path to action in understanding the job of the marketeer is to grease the wheels, to make it easier for the potential consumer to buy. Know, Like and Trust is the best lubricant in marketing we will ever have. If people know you, like you and trust you, and preferably really LOVE you, a lot of your marketing can be as simple and easy as reminding people to buy again.

KLT is built over time. Sure, people may *like* you immediately, but that doesn't mean they know and trust you, let alone love you – not yet.

The smart way to build KLT is to enhance your marketing with something they already do know, like and trust, maybe a joint venture with a recognized brand. Look at the film and TV industries – casting actors that people already know, like and trust when you're making a film turbo-charges the chances of the consumer buying tickets to see it. That's why famous, popular actors get paid so much.

With content marketing, which I do, I give information away for free to build up a KLT before I ask for any business. We've tracked our customers, and in some cases they have watched our videos and read my books for months and years before they've done business with us. That content greased the wheels ready for us to make a sale.

Value beats price

When value beats price, people will often skip past their usual buyer protection process and buy immediately. If they like the product or service but don't see ultimate value, they'll make excuses to put off the purchase. The most popular one has to be 'I'll ask my husband/wife'. That just means they are not yet 100% sure they want to buy. They may not even have a husband/wife!

Overwhelming value over price is a cure for 'buyer's remorse' – the feeling we get after buying something when we weren't really sure we wanted it. Buyer's remorse can happen to anyone, regardless of wealth. Smart marketeers know that they need to prevent buyer's remorse by greasing the wheels before the sale and remind the customers what a great decision they have made after the sale too.

If you can offer enough value compared with the price, common sense kicks in – *I must buy this now*. The trick is to lock in this added value with a call to action to act now.

The call to action

Getting a customer to act NOW and not put off the sale to another day is essential for results. *Never forget that people forget. Research states that as people we have between 20,000 and 70,000 thoughts a day and if action isn't taken immediately then lots of other thoughts fill that space.* That's a vital part of a marketeer's success plan. Hence the importance of the CTA – the call to action.

Humans are programmed to avoid missing out on opportunities, so we must weave this into our marketing by creating a feeling of urgency – the need to act now or lose out.

Remember also that we humans at large copy-buy. If someone else whose judgment we value says a product is good, we buy it too, because it reduces the risk in the purchasing decision. Hence branding.

We also buy what others buy because we want to BE like them. This copycat buying starts when we are just kids. Even young children learn to copy the other kids by wearing the same brands or riding the same bikes, because it makes them feel that they belong to the in-crowd. Understanding this is a powerful weapon in marketing.

These ideas have given me a number of thoughts on creating a call to action.

The greatest companies and brands train their customers to do business on the terms they want. Here's a few examples:

Pre-buy list

This means putting your name on a pre-launch list ahead of time, agreeing to buy before the product is available. This method can create more desire for the product by making sure it sells out soon after launch (in most cases it can be made available again). This is what happens with products affected by import restrictions or supply issues, like fine wine from a good vintage.

Limited supply

Limited supply that's real and not just pretend really does get people to buy. If you market a product that tends to sell out because of limited supply, like a fashion product that's only made in limited numbers, you create a surge of unsatisfied desire. I know restaurants that tell people they're fully booked to create a buzz and urgency, making people believe that this is the in-place to eat and they'd better book a table fast if they want to join in. Concert promoters don't release all the tickets when a tour is first announced, which allows them to create the illusion that there are hardly any seats left, so you'd better book right now or you won't get to see your favourite band. I know someone who booked tickets for the 2019 Eagles UK tour back in October 2018 because the website suggested that nearly all the tickets had already sold out. Six months later tickets for most of the dates were still available – and the price had come down! They increase the pressure by using on-line booking systems that give you just a short window of a few minutes to press 'buy' before your precious tickets go back on sale to the rest of the world again.

How can you create limited supply? I tell people that the last time we did this, we sold out in so many days.

Wanting to buy what you can't have

Everyone wants to buy today what they can't get until tomorrow – we're wired to want what we can't have. Apple are the masters of this. They show products at their conferences that will not be available for another year. That creates an unsatisfied longing.

I love doing this in our companies. Previewing what's coming before your customers can buy it creates an immediate surge of desire for your products, and instant customers ready for when they are available.

'The price will go up!'

My experience has shown that this really works. Everyone knows that in the long term house prices only ever go up, so the sooner they buy the better. But it doesn't have to be just houses. Rolex put their prices up every year for the same product, which means people who desire the brand have learned that the watch they want can only be more expensive in the future. But you have to be true to your promise or people will soon rumble you – no good promising price increases and then cutting them, or you will lose trust. With expensive, desirable products, like watches, cars and hi-tech cameras, people may watch prices for months before buying, so they know the truth.

Free trials, and try before you buy

A free limited trial that is clearly marketed as once in a lifetime, or even free for the first 30 days, also gets people to take action. I am a huge fan of using free offers to get a customer. In my opinion this trumps discounting every time.

We never expect free forever, but we do expect discounts forever, once we've got them

All these points come down to limited time. When you put a time limit on your call to action, either 'buy now or never again' or pre-planning a time-limited offer, or if you don't buy this time you'll have to pay more, motivate people to take action.

REMEMBER: Never forget that people forget.

Articles – the advertorial

Who better to explain what an advertorial is than Wikipedia:

An **advertorial** is an ad in the form of editorial content. In printed *publications, the advertisement is usually written to resemble an objective article and designed to ostensibly look like a legitimate and independent news story. In television, the advertisement is similar to a short infomercial presentation of products or services. These can either be in the form of a television commercial or as a segment on a talk show or variety show. In radio, these can take the form of a radio commercial or a discussion between the announcer and representative. The concept of internet-based advertorials is linked to native advertising; however, whether the two terms are synonymous is a point of discussion.*

Whenever we put ads in publications, we have one rule: **We must have an article in the media to go alongside it**. This gives the ad so much more power. Preferably we ask the journalist to write the piece for us, but knowing how overworked they are, we would always send an article in too. These days the print media are struggling for circulation and profits, so they often rely on a tiny editorial staff and don't have the capacity to write all the material they need to fill each edition.

Let me clarify this with a scenario. Suppose I am placing an ad for a cookery book, called say 'Meals to Impress in 15 Minutes', because I want to get it out into the world and get my grubby hands on some sales to remunerate me for my efforts. I would accompany that ad with an article and a recipe from the book.

Backing up an ad like this works best if the editorial part is seen as separate from the ad, so it has the extra credibility of being part of the journalistic content. So make sure it doesn't *look* like an ad – make it factual and helpful, and only plug the book at the end.

Exhibitions

Exhibitions are expensive – in floor and service charges, materials and manpower. It's only worth paying the ridiculous money they demand to show your wares if you can have a speaking slot or five – yes, I really do mean five – so you can be the most famous face at the event.

When called to speak at a conference, I always tell them they can have my speaking session at a discount in return for a free stand. I will then also tell people I am speaking there. Being a speaker means you'll be all over the show programme, and also that you'll be seen as an authority. Whenever I speak at exhibitions, my stands are full to the brim after each talk. I am pulling leads, not pushing for them.

TOP TIP: Your talk must have a great problem-solving title, to grab attendees at a conference exhibition to come to you.

For example: 'How a clown built a business doing a million pounds in a year, and how you can too.

Social posts, with headings and questions

As with advertorials, I have found long-form social posts can sometimes be a great way of pulling people towards you, especially if they're in the right groups. The trick is to build a following on social media, and the smaller the following the better this works. Be honest and truthful in your post – give real value. At the end you can invite people to find out more by sending you a private message.

Example:

HEADING: I just spent £20,000 on Linked In ads – I'm furious, how can they do that! (This is the A in AIDA).

> **Middle** - How this happened and just how good it was.

> **End** - If you'd like a free call with me to show you how. This then gets you a client.

Make me an offer – today only.

Occasionally, and I mean once a year or twice at most, I put a message out on social media that you can make me an offer for any of our companies to do business with you, or even have 1:1 time or mentoring with me. You'll need a little following to make this work, so effort is needed in creating content in the first instance.

I say on video, 'You make us an offer and we will either accept or make a counter offer'. Once you have an audience of some sort, you'll get offers very quickly. This also captures the warm leads, the people who just needed a nudge to take action.

The rules

- There must be a deadline. It has to be done today, or by the end of the week/month etc, because that's when the offer ends.
- After the deadline you'll still get offer messages. You must reply that the deadline is up and will be repeated on a future date, and offers can be submitted then. This confirms your credibility, trains your customer to be responsive and gives loyalty to the ones who took action in time.

From followers to fans

There are two ways to get profit from your marketing and you can now do both. I often teach these two ways to get customers in the form of two pyramids – see the diagram below. From the original pyramid scheme business model, this is still applicable and relevant to the way we buy from companies today, but in a more developed way.

Followers to Fans - few do this

Years ago some smart companies, like Disney, realised that if you had followers who watched TV shows, music or films, then once the prospect had consumed the content you could kick the profit down the road through, for example, buying the toys or visiting the theme parks. This speeds the process, not just to getting customers but advocates and fans very quickly – far more quickly than the other option used by the many.

Sport does the same. Once you consume the content (the games), you're a fully signed-up fan buying tickets, clothes and memorabilia.

Searchers to Fans - most do this

Searchers to Fans is what most people did and still do – they market tripwire products like the methods in this book. In my diagram I call this 'shoppers looking for offers'. At first sale, they become customers.

Trouble is, customers are fickle – they can be lured away by a competitor's offer. The trick is to get the customer to consume your service at least four times. This is when habit kicks in and loyalty grows. My view is that we need to make our customers feel like members, even if it's not a traditional membership business. People are proud to be a member of something.

Frankly, religions have been doing this for years – very successfully, because we all want to belong. Being a member of a political party, a golf club, a gym or a visitor attraction are examples of the ones we think of, but it doesn't stop there. Think how successful Amex are at making credit card users feel like members, how good the wholesalers Costco are at making their customers feel proud to be members. Once you identify as a member, you become blind to offers from competitors – you're a member of a community now, and loyalty kicks in.

Advocates – people who recommend you – are members on steroids for your business. They are hugely important. But advocates are not quite fans, and it's important to remember that. You'll have a lot more advocates than fans, and that's OK. Here's the big difference: when asked, advocates will recommend you proudly and confidently, while fans go around telling people about you even if they're not asked. This is the power football fans have for their teams.

If you look at my two diagrams below showing how to get people to be fans, you'll notice everything is the same except the bottom of the pyramid. You'll either have to convince shoppers to become customers with marketing, or you can get people to be followers first. In reality, in my companies we do both.

This followers-to-fans revolution – how do you achieve it?

I say 'revolution' because believe me, we're in a world where the small-time marketeer can now seriously compete and have a huge impact. This is great news. Never before was it possible.

We live in a digital age, and luckily for the small business, this means we can now create content to get followers and compete on both options.

When I compare our tiny little company to Disney and know that we both use the same route to get a customer, it gives me the same goosebumps I've felt on a first date with the girl I thought I'd never get! We both use the content marketing route. We have now seen success in our own small way.

I get excited for two reasons:

1. Marketing to someone who's seen your content is so much easier.

2. Being branded/trusted is now possible. The GREAT news is we can create the content. The really SPIFFING news is we have the platforms for it too (YouTube, Facebook, Linked In etc). This is the

game changer. Years ago you could have created the content, but you needed the strength of Hercules to persuade anyone to put it on the limited platforms available.

Members are like a marketing department that you're not paying for.

Making your customers feel like members and giving them the opportunity to label themselves as such could quite possibly be the answer to the question all entrepreneurs get asked...

What's the one thing you know now that you wished you'd known when you started?

Or the classic...

What would you write to your 18-year-old self starting out?

The answer is – build your company so your customers feel like they have membership with you. We've been involved in start-up membership businesses that have been built as such by design, the smart approach for sure. One of the best things about experience is knowing what will work and what will not; the worst thing is knowing that most things don't work and having protection that stops you trying new stuff.

Since I discovered this treasure of treasures, we have re-engineered our companies to get members. My team know I am now obsessed with memberships. Members allow you to predict income and cash flow more easily - the stressbuster of business.

The better news is they're like your FREE outsourced marketing department, willing to bring their nearest and dearest to the front door of the shop.

Members create members – they want to bring people to the community. The better news is that members' friends and families will probably like your business, because they are like the already initiated member.

I signed up to Amex, and I'm a fan. My friend Mark is a member, but he's more than a member, he's a super member. He knows all the proprietary language used by members of the clan. You'd think he owned the thing, or at the very least had a big chunk of shares with a seat on the board – he's like Mr Amex. It was he who indoctrinated me.

You'll all have met a Mark in your walk through life. He spends a good deal of his free time at BBQs and gatherings, telling people how much he loves Amex and the benefits. He loves to tell his listening audience that he flies round the world first class for £6.50 a time. Mark is his company's top salesman in the Midlands. Apparently the CEO tried to give him a bonus and an award at their staff get-together for top salesmen for new memberships. To the CEO's disappointment, he was told Mark wasn't even on the payroll.... I jest, but this is the power of making your customers feel like members. They become your outsourced marketing department. After all, wouldn't we all want people sharing stories about your company at family gatherings and BBQs? That, my friends, gets more customers... sorry, members.

Throw one ball at a time

If you throw 10 balls the customer will only catch one – maybe none.

I wish this phrase was my invention. Alas no, it comes from one of our senior team members, Lyssa Elster. I love Lyssa and the skills she's brought to the table. She gets the broader sense of marketing and she's a damn fine copywriter.

Lyssa's keynote phrase when discussing an approach in the business is 'playing devil's avocado'. It always makes me laugh, and I suppose it also makes me think twice. After all, we must always try and take on multiple views before deciding the correct approach. You'll need a Lyssa in your dream team if you want to win long term.

When crafting marketing, if we throw too many messages, our prospect gets confused and will forget everything. Too many messages is a great temptation to the uninitiated in marketing, who are tempted to throw every possible solution you offer to the prospect. This just stops any decision being made. Throw them one and they are bound to catch it.

I remember a story a very wealthy man told me. He started out as an estate agent and died one of the wealthiest men I knew. After World War 2 the need for housing was huge, and of course this was way before the internet could allow you to work from home and live where you wanted. Prospects would come to his office looking for houses to buy. He'd take them to see at least 10, but they could never make a decision and as a result his sales were always low.

Then one day he decided to lie. Prospects came to his office as normal, but this time, he said he only had two houses for sale, and then when they had viewed them he would ask which one they wanted. His sales went through the roof, and helped to start him off on his path to riches.

So if in your marketing you say you do this, and this, and this, and this and this... they won't do any of them, and you'll leave with nothing.

That's why I say that if you throw ten balls at your customers, there's a chance they won't catch any of them.

Chapter 5
The customer journey

Crafting a plan for your ideal customer journey will create a valuable business. My best successes have been when we've offered something for free or very low cost, to get people to try before they buy - to try YOU, not the individual product. As explained earlier, this is your MOST customer, which you need in order to find your IDEAL customer.

The sales funnel

Here's our sales funnel for our leisure business:

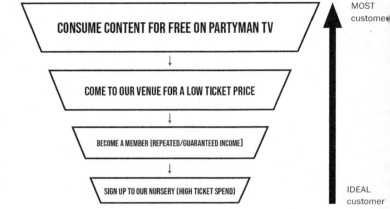

So we build 'know, like and trust' by offering free content, then marketing low-value tickets to our venues for great days out, then converting to memberships, which have a higher average customer value, and then into our nursery, which has the highest value. We throw one ball at a time. We market what we do, and we understand the customers' value to us once we understand their journey with us.

TOP TIP: On the content to relations journey – never ask for sex on the first date!

Why the money is ALL in the list

Marketeers who are in the know belong to their own little clique, like all of us in communities, and we too have our own proprietary language. Being no different from any other clique, we have our own name for a customer database – the 'list'. It doesn't matter what you call your list – you just need to have one, if you are going to have any chance of keeping customers and getting them to come back to you again and again.

Something we didn't do when we started out, and for some years after we started, was to invest time in building a great list of customer numbers, emails, buying history and addresses. So, so stupid! I feel cross just writing it. The amount of money we left on the table is quite frankly shocking. Don't be like me. Build your database and keep it alive and current. Fortunately we now know this, so we work hard to keep our list alive.

The basic function of all marketing is to build a list and stay friends with it. You don't just sell to it, you create a relationship with it. Then when you want to sell, you just remind your customers to do business with you. It really is that simple.

If over time, you build a database of 10,000 people and then send out a letter with some killer copy and a brilliant call to action and they respond, you're singing merrily all the way to the bank.

Keep building your database and you'll build huge value. Remember companies have sold for millions based on the strength of their database.

Building your list - top tips

1. Make it cultural

If you want a real live database, the essence of database building (actually getting customers' details) is not putting in snazzy software but making it part of team culture. This is so important for the database to grow. You want your team to get behind the importance of it and enjoy seeing the results.

The building of a database has become harder with GDPR (General Data Protection Regulation) in the UK, especially for the direct-to-consumer market, but asking permission is still worthwhile, and proper effort to database building is essential.

We ask permission and sell the pain we can save people if they are on our database. It is even better to get your customers to become members so they believe in being part of your 'family'. You must create ways to promote being in the database on the basis of the pain it will save.

Let me share the story of Dave and the golf course.

Dave had a golf course – a crazy golf course, naturally. Half his customers booked to play in advance on his website, and he had the data neatly stored in the database, self-filled by customers – this is the way most companies fill their databases.

For me as his mentor, I was asking, what about the walk-ups, those who didn't book? That was tens of thousands of people, all of whom could be invited to repeat buy, yet Dave didn't know who they were! We needed to create a system to get them back.

So here's what we did. Knowing people are lazy with filling out forms and skip past the bits they can't be bothered with – you know how annoying it is to have to fill something out – we created a text sequence.

We also knew that half the data was wrong and we needed to add it to a system rather than relying on people to gather it, which is slapdash at best.

We said to walk-up paying customers, 'If you'd like a free game after the one you've paid for we have a voucher available. Text 'GOLF' to 123456 and the voucher will be sent to you.' The customers were overjoyed! And so were we, because now we had their mobile numbers. In the text we asked for their email, so we could send them the voucher – brilliant data for the database of actual, real customers. Then in the future we could send them offers to encourage them to come back.

Text messages are quick and easy ways to build data. To find out how to do this in detail, search for Text Message Marketing, James Sinclair on my YouTube channel.

2. Use text messages

Text messages are a great way to build a database. Better than that, they have huge open rates compared to email. At the time of writing they have an 80% open rate with a 40% click through.

In the database creation process, customer journeys must be simple.

Let's give another example. If I talk at an event, I'll say, 'If you'd like a free copy of my book text 'James' to 66777 and we'll send it to you'. This journey then happens:

Hi, what's your name?

They give their name.

We then say; Great, what's your email?

They give their email.

Brilliant, we'll send you a link to request your free book. In the meantime, subscribe to James' YouTube channel for some amazing content to set you going.

The result: lovely accurate data that we can see and make friends with.

TOP TIP in database building: At the point of transaction, ask.

This is so simple – the lowest-hanging fruit, but most just don't do it. Will you?

Buy data, and defrost the people from it

There are many places where you can buy detailed data for the industries you operate, and a quick Google search will bring you a menu to choose from. It's worth going à la carte and paying a bit extra so you can hammer down on exactly who you want to reach. This works really well in the B2B world.

It's smart to get a list of people who will be more likely to buy what you sell, rather than going to the masses. This sounds simple and it is, but the real work, which most do not do, is communicating with your new database and making friends with it. That is the real magic in making this work.

Most people start a new diet, buy the plan and then do nothing. Don't do that. Make friends with your new database

This process of communicating with data means you'll have a frosty reception initially, like trying to chat someone up in the street, so you'll need to warm things up. Do not try to sell to it straight away. First you must try to defrost the relationship. When we've bought data, we've simply started by giving great free advice and tracked opening rates and clickthroughs. We then give more. We've given my books, sent my videos and my podcasts to try to start a relationship, even invited people to free seminars.

The process is give, give, give and THEN ask them to be customers – not to ask straight away.

TOP TIP: When it comes to buying data, you don't want to be throwing mud at the wall and hoping some of it sticks. Choose your data well.

Reviews and testimonials

Because someone else talking about you positively beats you talking about you.

Testimonial marketing is quite possibly my favourite form of marketing. It's free and rarely used to its full beautiful advantage. Free it is, but effort it needs. It's like using good old word of mouth as a way of getting customers, but it's word of mouth on steroids.

Getting word of mouth out there can be improved, increased and implemented by the business that has put a plan in place to make it happen. You can create a system to get people to talk about you – we've done this in our companies many times.

Adding a testimonial or two from satisfied customers is mega powerful in getting new customers. Alternatively we can get endorsement from a celebrity they'll know or a recognized local company. Your testimonial needs to be REAL.

Online you can add reviews – in fact you MUST add reviews. They are immensely powerful in getting customers, on Trip Advisor, Trustpilot, Amazon and so many other places – lots of people wouldn't think of booking a restaurant or a holiday now without checking what their customers have been saying about them. Good reviews on Google will send your search engine ratings through the roof. So ask your happy customers (which I hope is most of them) to review you. Just about every group of people has a Facebook group now – cyclists, lawyers, model railway enthusiasts, birdwatchers, carp fishermen, koi carp breeders, caravanners, even play centre owners belong to one. If a member of a group gives you a good review, all the other members will want to be your customer.

On social media we ask people with big followings to come and have a day out for free and tell their followers how much they loved our business. We then share this testimonial with the world.

Simple system 1

The system doesn't have to be complicated. The simple ones are always the best. For example, we have asked people who have had a day out at one of our attractions to leave us a review, if they've had a good time. We don't leave this to chance; after they've been, we send an email with the link to a review site. We also give out cards on the way home directing them where to go to leave a testimonial.

Simple system 2

We interview customers and put together a whole video asking people what they think, then share this through our marketing channels. Sharing these testimonials on video is the smartest bit of business you can do.

The big boys' logo on your marketing

We love to tell the world what testimonial/review sites are saying about us. The Trip Advisor award endorsing us and our 5-star Google reviews have always helped in pushing us forward.

On websites you can now get software that shows real positive reviews from review sites scrolling across your site.

Awards

Closely linked to testimonials, awards give prospects the comfort they need to do business with you. Getting an award should be celebrated – not because you've won it, but because it means people will talk about you and do business with you.

Every time we've won awards we've shared the news with our prospects and our existing customer base to remind them to come back to us. We've lapped up all the attention and communicated with all the other businesses in the room at award dos in our hunt for prospects and leads.

Awards means other companies at awards find you, hear about you and share synergy with you, because they are your fellow finalists. Business awards have sponsors, delegates and entries and press attention – your job is to make sure they all know about you.

Note: Get someone who's amazing at copy and putting together awards to help produce a great award pack.

Be unusual

Marketing is all about sticking out from the norm: it's all about getting attention. The more unusual you are, the more attention you'll get, because most business owners just do what the rest of the market is doing. That's why we discussed off-line marketing. Fewer and fewer people are participating in off-line marketing, choosing to use the crowded on-line world as their first point of call. If you've got the money to write the cheque, this does work, but if you want to leverage your pennies, then off-line can help.

How can you be unusual? That's the question everyone asks me. It's simple, I say. I have dressed as dinosaurs and worn purple tuxedos at industry events to get our companies noticed. If you saw a giant purple dinosaur at a swanky awards do, that was someone getting noticed. Cost – free.

We once covered a vehicle in very realistic fake snow sourced from a film production company, then parked it up on the side of the road to market our Father Christmas event at one of our attractions. We nearly caused a serious traffic jam as people tried to understand how only that vehicle was covered in snow and it wasn't anywhere else. The council wasn't happy.

The cost was minimal. The eyeballs on us? Lots.

We have made videos every day and given away all the best stuff we know for free, when everyone else charges. It's unusual to do this. Sure, the ROI is longer but in the long run the payback is so much more than paid-for advertising.

I know my seminars have changed business people's lives. One person who came to my free taster business seminar told the world on Facebook that they felt guilty for being there for free. It's unusual, so we win.

I think being unusual can be as simple as making it easy for your customer to contact you. The effort you have to make to speak to someone or find the number you need on a company website baffles me at times. Don't make it so people need a degree in neuroscience to contact your company. That's stupid.

TOP TIP: *Being extraordinary in an ordinary world is a good way to win in marketing YOUR business.*

The best book you'll ever read is the one you wrote

As the author of three business books and counting, I will let you into a little secret. I feel a bit of a fraud. Writing is not part of my natural skill set, so my books have been through a diligent editing process. They were all my words, just not necessarily in the right order – until an editor stepped in. They are a real effort for me to do and they take time, but boy are they worth it.

Being on stage, podcasts and video are different. I find my happy place here, and I can do it with complete ease. So why books? I think they open doors, boost credibility, allow your reader to build an understanding of you; this creates trust. **Trust is gold dust when it comes to getting customers.**

Authors have authority, and it's no surprise that the words are so closely related. If you have authority, you'll open doors.

My books have got me on stages at conferences to speak to thousands of leads at a time, and won me hot, ready-to-buy clients – clients who call me when I never even knew them.

My books have got me onto radio stations, found me business partners, joint venture clients and even funding. It gets better than that; they have allowed me to communicate my clear vision for how to do things with people who have come to work with me.

Books for your business niche will get you customers. They are a lead magnet of epic power. Before you think, 'hang on James, I'm not JK Rowling, or Stephen King, or John Grisham,' you have to write a book about what you know, and it won't be fantasy fiction.

I find the easiest way to structure a book is to prepare a keynote presentation about what I'm going to say in its pages. Start with an intro, then compose a set of slides with headings (these will be your chapters). You then talk about the headings of each slide (chapter content) and finally you come to a conclusion – same as a book. It's a quick and easy way to plan it out. The structure is the task. To turn it into a well-ordered page-turner of a book you need to seek the help of a talented copywriter – as I did.

You MUST have a premium price product!

Time and time again I have learnt this and we as business owners/ marketeers should never forget it. I have seen this in my own behaviour as a consumer too.

If you own an airline and you didn't offer first class, you'll lose customers to a rival.

If you own a hotel and don't have suites, you'll lose customers.

Some people want to go straight to the top and pay top whack – it's just how they're programmed.

I hate queuing, really HATE it. I will happily pay to jump the queue and win time back. If you don't offer that choice to me, I'll go elsewhere. I want to pay more on some things, and if you don't offer it... off I go.

You will have customers who will just pay more. Make sure you cater for this small group, because there's a good chance they're the people that love you the most too.

Chapter 6
Reaching your customers

Tried & tested vs. new & unspoilt

In choosing your marketing approach, you need to be aware of a sad fact – marketeers ruin everything. It's true – TV was great until commercials came along on every channel except the BBC, and you have to pay for that. Then the same thing happened to radio. You can't watch your favourite band on YouTube without sitting through an ad at the beginning. The more marketeers catch on to a new media channel, the more they spoil it for the rest of us. Who needs marketeers?

Well, you do. But you need to make sure that YOUR marketeers are always thinking round the corner. If everyone's getting fed up of ads on Facebook, look at Twitter. If email isn't working, think about using texts – open rates on email have fallen to tiny, but 80% of texts are still being read. A PR consultant I know sent out his first email shot when he started in business 20 years ago. He emailed 100 local businesses, and got enough work to last him for a year. Now he's lucky to get one little piece of work from 1000 emails. We've all become almost email-proof.

So when responses are falling, ask yourself what's going to be the next communication channel that hasn't been spoiled yet.

The internet and social media are getting busier and busier, noisier and noisier, every week. So don't assume that marketing is all about online – it never was and it never will be.

My favourite marketing methods

Here's a rundown of the marketing methods I have tried. There are others, but I won't mention those because I can't speak from experience. I have tested all the ones I've covered. For the benefit of this section, I've stripped back things that don't appear to have worked for me in the quest to get customers *easily* - and easily is the key word here.

Radio

I've spent a fair amount on radio – enough to buy a house in fact – but I think in hindsight that money would have been better spent elsewhere to get customers. That said, radio has been proved to work and as part of a marketing mix when budgets are big, I believe that like TV it has its place. Radio works best when it's part of a huge multi-million-pound cross-marketing budget used in conjunction with other media. You need to go big or go home. Radio is not guerrilla marketing, it's broad marketing and for us, Guerrilla Marketing is our weapon of choice in the art of getting customers.

The following are my easy wins, the lowest hanging fruits, the walk before you run, the menu of the day, the bread and butter that I always turn to.

Joint ventures and collaborations

Leveraging another database or collection of customers has launched some businesses from zero to hero, overnight in some cases. It takes years to build trust, and a joint venture (JV) with a company that has trust, but doesn't offer what your service offers, may save all that time. We've done plenty of these arrangements to get things cooking quicker. Conversely, plenty of other businesses would like to leverage your experience and skills so they can quickly add some revenue with minimal work. They get you the customers, you service them.

So many people think you have to go big on a joint venture, but it just isn't the case. You don't have to go into full-on business with someone – you can just do one-offs, dip your toe.

The best JVs are those bringing together contrasting skill sets, as this gives benefits to both sides and creates mutual respect.

Lead magnets

A lead magnet does what it says on the tin – it's an idea that attracts leads. This could be a book, a video or a free 'How to Guide', or a chance to try something for free. Lead magnets work beautifully on social media such as Facebook.

The best way to think of them is that they create an irresistible 'ethical inducement', offering something valuable that the prospect wants in exchange for their contact details (the lead). My best lead magnets have always been copies of my books.

The lead magnet must be consumed by the prospect to turn them from lead to shopper.

Here are some of the lead magnets we've created:

- Video Courses

A 4-part video series that gives a breakdown of information has always been a winner in terms of building a database. I have used this method many times to create success.

- Email or e-courses

Creating a e-course that is based online through your Customer Relationship Management (CRM) system is a great way to harness the non-watchers – we all consume differently.

Make sure your CRM system ties in with a lead score. A good CRM will rank the readership and score of the action taken.

- eBooks

People do find these of value and they remove the trickery of emails and e-courses above. People instantly know the value of a book.

- Books

When I speak, I sometimes offer my book in return for your business card. The leads generated have amounted to tens of thousands of pounds.

- Checklists

People love to download, checklists and blueprints and check the points off. In return you get yourself a lead.

Think of it like this – giving is the start of receiving. The lead magnet needs a value, such as a useful or desirable gift.

Industry organisations

Industry organisations cement my belief in the phrase 'riches in niches'. These puppies have landed me millions of pounds worth of sales and even bigger opportunities. If you want to acquire businesses with ready-made customers for little or no capital, this is the place to hang about. Speak at their meetings, make friends with them, join the committees and get known.

I have been shocked by how many people look to exit their businesses and wish to hand them over to people who will look after their customers once they've had enough. So many people want out of their businesses, but they're much harder to sell than you'd think.

I teach the process of how to do this at my Entrepreneurs' Masterclass. They can catapult business growth with little or no money down.

I joined leisure organisations, and through these groups I met customers for the products we manufacture for their leisure businesses. Because we were in the same game, we had synergy and relatability. I have also bought companies from them with no money down or taken over sites they no longer wanted, and you guessed it – they came with customers.

Organisations for customers

If you're in the Business to Business (B2B) world you'll also find plenty of customers, networks and similar businesses that may recommend you for the services/products/things which they don't do themselves.

Teddy Tastic, our make-a-bear company, which has enjoyed millions of pounds' worth of sales, was a start-up built from scratch, through us as a company going to leisure trade organisations and the events they put on. We networked with the people in the room and built rapport. This takes time, but over time the dividends are hugely worthwhile.

There will be trade organisations for every business niche you can think off. Go hunt them down and become famous to a few in those niches, then watch the customers rat-a-tat-tat on your door.

100% money back guarantee

Our companies always want to do the right thing. We're proud of that fact. We want people to absolutely love buying from us, and if they're not we've always gone and bent over backwards to put things right or make people happy. So if that's your mindset, as it is for most great business owners, tell people – especially if they are new prospects. Offer money back guarantees. In many cases that's the little push the new prospect needs to step over the line to being a customer.

The power of email

Email is still one of our top go-to strategies for getting customers. It baffles me how this low-effort marketing tool is just not used at all by so many businesses, while at the other extreme, some firms use it as the only way to get customers. It gets worse, because so many are useless at it. There are so many little wins to be made in increasing your results from emails - some of which I will share with you here.

Avoiding the email cull

In most cases email open rates are falling as we consumers get more efficient with our daily email cull ritual: delete, delete, delete, block sender... I do it, and I'm sure you do too. The trick is to work out how to avoid the cull and get noticed. It comes down to testing and measuring. A few quick pointers below can massively increase your open rates and click throughs (open rate is the opening of the emails, click through is the reader clicking to do what you're asking them to do in the email).

Above all we need to get your email opened and people clicking where we want them to.

Subject line is crucial, critical. It is the life blood of your campaign, closely followed by clicks in the email.

Use multiple clickthroughs! Buttons, videos, hyperlinks, more buttons, more hyperlinks – they all give you more chance of clickthroughs happening.

Don't let your customer get lost. The punter's motto for shopping on websites is 'If at first you don't succeed... give up and try another site'. Any confusion and they click off your site and look somewhere else. Don't make it a pirate's treasure map, with one X marks the spot to get the treasure – leave lots of Xs, so it's as easy as possible for the reader to action a click through.

For example, you know your link is to a video, but do they? Is the play button really obvious? Use the familiar language and symbols of the internet, such as an arrow 'play' icon – don't be clever or different, you'll only confuse people, particularly those who are not so internet savvy.

The big red button that says 'PRESS HERE' gets a thumbs up from me. Just because you know doesn't mean they'll know. You are not your customer. **Keep It Simple Stupid!**

Email dos and don'ts

Let's recap on the best ways to increase your email effectiveness.

Subject line – you really need to think about ideas and wording that will capture attention and make someone want to open the email. Set deadlines, ask questions, arouse curiosity. If possible, add the person's name. This is a good one: *'James, have I upset you?'*

Emojis – Use these in the subject line. If your prospect is getting 100 emails a day and yours is the only one with an emoji in the title, you will stick out.

Send it from a person. The open rate is always better when it comes from a person, so put 'Mike at Marsh Farm' rather than just 'Marsh Farm'.

Preview subject line – Add wording to this rather than leaving it blank. You can do this on your email software.

Send time – First thing in the morning and last thing in the day, people go through and delete loads of emails, so send yours after these 'purge' times.

Links on email - Have multiple places/links in the email where customers can click to book/buy. I'd say at least 4, but always try for more, 6 or 7 and you're more likely be in customer-getting heaven.

Images – when embedding a thumbnail for a video, have the play button in the artwork as well as the link.

Vouchers, coupons and leveraging other people's customers

I see offering vouchers as a mini joint venture with other lists. If you can cross-promote then the effectiveness of the campaign will increase, as both parties put in more effort. It's a you-scratch-my-back-I'll-scratch-yours way of marketing. We look to partner with organisations, businesses and communities who have followings, or – as you're now initiated in the art of getting customers – what we call 'hot lists' that you can identify and which fit your customer avatar.

In our companies, we get on the good old dog and bone and dial those digits, to organisations that have a similar customer base to us. We build relationships by making exclusive offers on our products and services to their lists.

We have a great hit rate in terms of success in these distribution channels. For us we like to think of it as cheap direct mail. For example in the case of our family visitor attractions, we specifically target schools in our age bracket, as they're our perfect customer avatar.

Getting your message out through organisations that fit your customer base is smart. It also looks like an endorsement for your services. For us, when a school is giving out our leaflets we get brand association with that specific community brand. Remember: BRAND = TRUST.

We've even structured it so they distribute our vouchers to their customers for us, in this case students. We have never paid for it. We call this 'cross marketing' – the students get a discount and we get customers. Instead of paying for this we give free gifts in terms of free entry or services.

We've sent literally millions of vouchers from our companies. What I love about them is you get two great things:

1. Data

The smart thing to do on a voucher is to try and get data. The discount you attribute to the voucher, maybe a cut-price offer or a discount, is therefore not an offer or a discount but a mechanism for you to buy data with no money down. If the voucher is used, we have that data. We can now make friends with the voucher user and direct market to them, knowing they've used us and have transacted with us before.

We try and get an email address and a name. The more data you can get, the more powerful it is.

2. Track and measure

When paying for coupons to go on print media, even if you're just paying for the print, it's important to have a way to track what's working and what's not. We can print in mass but add codes to certain areas of the leaflets to know what's worked and who's come from where.

One of our venues can have up to 50,000 vouchers a year returned, all from different places. The trick is that we know which those places are. We can then go hard on what's worked and drop what hasn't.

Car park tickets

Here's a thing: you park your car, you buy a windscreen parking ticket and on the back is an advert for a business. For the car park owner that's a sawdust business (a free by-product) and a sure thing for some research in the art of getting customers.

Yes, it's a voucher, but it's not free because you will have to pay the car park owners. It's not cheap, and most businesses just use it for awareness. Not us – as I said early, we don't pay for awareness marketing. Only a silly person would do that.

So how?

If you can turn a car park ticket into a voucher by printing on the back, then you can get some good returns, because you know by the redemption rate of those vouchers just how well the campaign worked.

I like it more because you can target paying car parks which you know are used by your customers, based on what's around the car park. For me local parks with families enjoying days out makes a lot of sense. So do cinema or leisure centre car parks.

Sure, there are more accurate ways of niching your customer avatar, but we have seen the campaign wash its face – pay for itself – when we've done it. Sometimes washing its face in acquisition marketing is good enough if you know you'll get your real profit further down the road. That's why knowing your customer value life journey or ALV (average life value) is crucial.

Newspaper competitions

Newspapers and magazines are taking a big dive in readership volumes unless they look after a niche, and often even then. The smart ones are adapting by going heavy online, but at the time of writing I believe that if you can get in for free with offers for their readers it's still worth a go.

Tracking phone numbers and unique links

You can set up and track different phone numbers for different response channels so you know where the enquiries have has come from. They can be either local or freephone numbers. This used to be a really expensive exercise, but they have become much cheaper. The numbers route callers to business phone numbers. Tracking numbers allow us marketeers to gauge the performance of specific marketing channels and/or campaigns as part of the call tracking process.

You could have a different number for your leaflets, online or in magazines. This gives you confidence in knowing where to place more ads for the future.

We can also use them with links and web domains to track where we've got our traffic from before going big where we know it will count.

Facebook and social media competitions

You now know that the aim is to get qualified eyeballs on your marketing. Social media platforms like Facebook allow you to go into their snazzy ad platform and pay for views from a demographic that are most likely to be interested in you. It's direct marketing and we like it.

Here's the other way that I try to do the same idea, but for free, or for as cheap as chips.

Social media platforms favour engagement (comments/likes/ shares) and if you get them naturally you'll stay prominent in people feeds, because the platform works out that people are liking what they see and they will continue to show your audience your content – that's what they want.

Once you have natural attention, it's down to your call to action to convert it! We do both, paid for and organic – so should you.

LET ME SAY THAT AGAIN... You want paid for and natural views. Let's discuss those natural views and how to get them; the algorithms favour interactions, they know that keeps people on their platform.

For example

- Comments
- Shares
- Tags
- Pausing on the post to read or view it (yes, they know that).

Facebook can be a great starting point for competition to achieve this too. You can have a contest that leads participants off Facebook and asks for actions there. Contest software with referral features that allow people to gain extra entries is permissible.

Here's a top tip:

1. Time limit the competition, so it doesn't make people wait to see if they win before they buy.
2. Make it a really decent prize, but one that's believable. At our visitor attractions, rather than a family pass as a prize we say, 'get 12 free tickets for your family and friends'.

Be unusual rather than usual. You don't want to be doing what everyone else is up to, and you'll find your reach goes that much further.

Hashtag comments

On LinkedIn, Instagram and all social media platforms, you can find a handy little harry called a search bar. In the search bar you can type a hashtag and subject around your industry to find people talking about your field or interests, for example #travelideas.

It's smart to get involved in this. For example, if you're a video editor looking to get customers or produce promotional videos, you could type #promovideo. A list of the most popular conversations come up, and that's your gold. You can comment, giving valuable advice and improvements ideas. This will attract people to follow you and voilà, the enquiries will come in. A figure of 50 a day will start the interest rolling, and it's free. It also builds audience.

Seriously – what's not to love?

Roadside signs

Roadside signs, if they are done well and there's enough of them, can send truckloads of people your way. In the past we've put up boards around our visitor attractions – we did 300 of them, so you couldn't drive anywhere without seeing them. They stuck out because they were unusual and out of place.

If signs are your next quest to get customers, remember KISS – Keep It Simple Stupid.

The fewer words the better. You've got time for a blink at best as people zoom along in their motor cars. Give the solution, not the features and benefits. The heading is all – no point in putting anything else in. No one is going to slow down, let alone stop the car to get out and read it! Though you could extend the message a little if you're able to put a sign at a junction where cars stop.

Our last sign was for our children's festival. It simply said this:

KIDS' FEST
AN AMAZING DAY OUT

We let the pictures around our heading tell the story so we didn't overword it. People take in pictures faster than words, as long as their message is clear and simple. When it comes to premises signs, I think the same applies. Your need, simple, bold, get-to-the-point signage.

Look at any small business tradesman and his van. Many of them cover the van with words covering every little thing they do, so none of it hits home and it's a waste of paint (or signwriting fees). Yesterday I saw a van which had four phone numbers on it and an email address. How are passing motorists going to use any of that? Your vehicle, or your sign, is not a business card – it's an attention-grabbing tool. Just give them something to google when they get home. So sad, so many opportunities lost.

Get in the car and go see the people

I'm a big advocate of getting in the car and going out to see people, actually talking to potential customers.Fewer and fewer people are doing this now.

On this topic, think about this – if you have customers who used to spend less with you than they used to, get in the car, go and see them and ask why. There may be a silly reason – like a new person has taken over purchasing and doesn't know about you, or they phoned you once with an order and didn't get through immediately so they went somewhere else, or they listened to a salesman and put their business elsewhere for no good reason, or they lost your contact details. Show up and explain that you should still be the go-to company for them, and you may get the lost business back there and then.

If you know of someone, or some business, that looks like your ideal customer, that could change your business, GO KNOCK ON THAT DOOR! I know a bank branch that drew up a list of all the businesses in its area whose business it wanted, then approached them all individually. That's the way to do it.

Salespeople

Great sales staff will literally pay for themselves time and time again. If you want the best from them, merge them into your products and services and get the right cultural fit. Do not do big basics, but be over-generous on commission. To make this work, make sure you have enough margin in your business so that you don't have to be tight with commission.

YouTube

YouTube is becoming more and more important to us in our companies as a marketing strategy. First things first: the amount of time people are spending on it increases continually. An average YouTube session is 40 minutes, compared to seconds on other social media platforms.

YouTube also notifies your regular viewers or subscribers when you upload new content.

YouTube ads, if done correctly, can be placed over content seen by the people who are most likely to buy from you because of similar content.

People want to buy what they can't buy

Understanding the buyer's psychology will help you greatly as a marketeer. We humans are strange creatures. If something is scarce, we want to buy because we're afraid of missing out or of being the only ones who don't have it. People want to buy Rolex watches. They don't need them – there are plenty of other watches that do just the same thing just as well – but Rolex, Breitling or Cartier watches are hard to buy because they're expensive, so owning one says something about you. As a rule of thumb, if we can't have something, we find we want it. Like when we go to a restaurant and they say something has sold out – suddenly that's the dish we want.

How do we use this? The smart thing is to carry on marketing until you're sold out, and tell people that. This will build up an unfulfilled desire for the product, and you'll get sales quicker when it's available again.

A friend of mine owns restaurants. When he opens a new one, he half-fills it in advance so that when people ring up and ask for a table they are turned away. This sends a message that you have to book earlier to get in.

Packages are beautiful

If you can think for customers so they don't have to, you should. This is something I really try to achieve. Our job is to make it easier for our shoppers to make decisions. If a customer wants some car polish, package it with a sponge and a chammy leather. If you're a music shop selling guitars, offer one complete with case, picks, spare strings and a how-to-play guide. Supermarkets love to do buy one, get another free or half price. The benefit of the saving is so obvious that customers will snap it up without thinking about it.

I prefer to give people packages that create a value-for-money feel which will start a buying habit, so they become returning customers. Create packages that give more value and you'll see the sales hopscotch to your bank account – but you *must protect margin.*

It can be as simple as offering an after-care service included in the package, or a series of bonuses that make the consumer feel like they've got a special deal.

The question I ask is – Are you giving your prospect a chance to brag about a deal they've had with you? BUT – you still protect the profit. It's all about amplifying value.

Example: Say you're a hotel. Rather than discounting room rates, add a package that includes champagne on arrival. The raw cost to you of a bottle of bubbly is a lot lower than knocking 20% off a room rate. Plus, discounted rates make you look desperate – as if no one wants to stay in your hotel.

Save thinking time for your prospect and you've got more chance of hopping them over the critical line from prospect to customer. Packages are also a great way of moving people from customer to advocate of your business, and it works faster if you factor in ways to spend more time with your business.

How? A hotel stay plus one-day spa day for you to return, then a week later a meal, then a further spa day for a special price. This package creates 4 transactions, and with that many transactions you've starting a habit. Remember – once you've used a business 4 times, you're in for the long run.

Video

Video is so important. We are now doing more of it than anything else in our quest to get customers and build a brand for our companies.

I will share next a little of our strategy on video. OK, these days we have our own video and content team, but I started with just a smartphone and a selfie stick.

Long form

Long-form video is brilliant for YouTube as it increases watch time, which YouTube loves, and if you get the views they'll reward you in their algorithm over time and give you yet more views.

So what is long-form video? Well, we film a whole seminar or a keynote talk from me, or an interview, which we then dual purpose, because we scrape the audio and turn it into a podcast.

We get greedy – we then chop the long form up into smaller videos. So one long-form keynote video could then become as many as 15 shorter videos on particular subjects. We love doing one set of work and then repurposing it.

Shareables

For the shorter videos we turn to shareables – these would be the ones that are most attention-grabbing for the flickers on social media. We understand that not many people are going to watch a full keynote presentation on Facebook as they would on YouTube.

We look for 60-second videos that we can add subtitles to. We then add a progress bar to show how long is left, and make it powerful to get a reaction. These are our two primary methods to increase brand and awareness.

Explainer videos

We also make a ton of these – in fact they are probably now the most important hack in getting customers using video. All businesses should be using explainer videos at the very least.

An explainer video should be short and sweet. It needs to explain just how fantastic your business is and quickly answer the silent questions people won't ask.

Learn to love cuts. Single-cut videos lose the viewers' interest, so keep it snappy and interesting, watch a TV show and count the cuts – you'll be shocked at just how many there are. They usually cut every 10 seconds, sometimes more.

Sales videos

A sales video should follow the AIDA (Attention, Interest, Desire, Action) formula and be like a sales letter in video format. Always get attention with your first sentence, then win the viewer's interest, then build desire, then give them a really clear and easy action to take to buy from you.

Podcasts

Sound is becoming a more and more important part of the media that people are consuming. This is great news for us in marketing awareness and creating enquiries for our companies.

Sound is available everywhere we go, with devices such as Alexa and Google Home. The world really is 'Alexa, play me a podcast on getting customers'. There you go – a feast for your ears.

This isn't science fiction, it's not a dream of the future – it's here right now. A podcast is a great way to build an audience, and it can quickly jump your profile from zero to hero. Just imagine all those juicy leads coming to you, all buyer ready.

We put full keynotes on podcasts, we go on other people's podcasts to gain new audiences and talk up our expertise – this has immediately delivered customers to us.

Podcasts are a great way to build relations with people. I love them because the podcast is leveraged work, meaning I do the podcast once and it keeps working, because people keep on listening and in turn customers keep coming.

Don't think you need a flashy studio and microphones that cost the world. It'll take time to build an audience, so get the idea before you get the gear. The gear is just the icing on the cake, adding refinement to your productions. Getting good at conversation and asking questions is far more important. You can upload your podcasts easily for free too.

Directories and maps

The internet is full of directories which you can usually list on for free, diarise to check up on them each year, so many come and go. If a directory is ranking high on search engines like Google, then it's worth paying for higher ranking.

Google have map listings that show you're an official business. It's free and it's imperative that if you have a physical location you submit your details to Google for natural free ranking on Google searches

Newsletters

Newsletters work great once you can tick your ACV, ATV and ALV boxes, because you know they are going to the people who are going to bring value to your business. A business I was involved in sent monthly newsletters, with great results. It took time, and they needed to be content rich and regular. They have to be monthly, and in my opinion, printed and sent in the post to really work. We made ours look like magazines, and the quality blew people away.

The big point is that they must teach, inform and harvest relationships, not sell. 80% value and 20% sales content was my primary aim.

It takes time, investment and cost to get a newsletter to your prospects. We spent £40,000 a year in print, post and packaging alone. So you need to make sure the cost is proportionate to the business.

For a newsletter to help you get customers you need to have a chance of high average customer value, the facility for the prospect to regularly transact and give you a good lifetime value. If you don't have all three, content marketing via email and video may be a better way to go.

A wealth management business ticks all three – it should absolutely send a newsletter or magazine to current clients and prospects. The ROI over time would pay dividends in growing your customers.

Leaflets

I love leaflets. Depending on your business, they can be the top trick to get you more customers, especially if you have a low ACV (average customer value). I've printed literally millions of leaflets.

With a leaflet, never forget a really strong and simple call to action. We always add a voucher or coupon so we can track success or indeed use tracking numbers (see Chapter 6). And don't forget those testimonials – at least one on every leaflet, designed to reflect what your ideal customer is looking for. Say you're selling home security and you know your customer really needs to feel safe in their home at night. The testimonial should say something like, 'My wife and I sleep like babies since we had an Alamo system fitted'. A name on the testimonial will make sure people know it's genuine. You'll need a system for collecting testimonials, from website surveys, emails, letters and the written word. Testimonials are a GREAT way to reassure customers that you really do deliver what you promise.

Distributing them is the money maker. Get them where your ideal customer is. We distribute to schools for our leisure business. If I was a takeaway or a local business I'd go through doors when people are least expecting it – early evening. 'What's just come through the door, love?' That's not what you say when the post arrives, but you would when you're brought something at 7pm.

Pay per click

We've paid to get clicks, and yes it works on search engines and on social media. This book is not going to delve massively into this – frankly, there are specialists who are better qualified than me to tell you how to do it. Seek the pros out and make sure the ROI stacks up before you get involved.

I have massively messed up PPC in the past - we've made money and lost it from PPC.

The single-shot web page

The smartypants marketeers call these 'squeeze pages'. I will call them what they are, so you can remember what I want you to achieve.

Once you've got a customer to your website or link, you want action. If you give them too much to do, there's a good chance they won't do any of it.

A squeeze page is a landing page designed to capture opt-in email addresses from potential subscribers or for your database. Its goal is to convince, cajole, or otherwise 'squeeze' a visitor into providing one of your most sought-after and coveted pieces of personal data: the email address, or buy what you have to offer in one sitting.

I have also used this method to sell tickets for our events. We don't mention everything we do because we know once they're a customer we can talk about that later.

Avoid mixing the message with all the stuff you do. Get the first transaction clear and the mixed messages you need to sell will be easier once you've got brand value with the customer.

Most websites have too many options. The one-action web page works best.

The old-fashioned appeal of direct mail and lumpy mail

I have left so much out when it comes to the wonderful stuff we can do with digital marketing. Why? Because I have always tried to make bigger impacts with offline marketing, because at heart that's where my comfort zone lies. That said, we do still love digital marketing – after all, the stuff works! But there are plenty of people far more qualified than me to take you through its ever-changing brilliance.

If that's what you really wanted to learn, then to disappoint you further, we're now going to wander down memory lane to the most un-digital media I know – snail mail, the good old post. It's now used less and less as the marketeer rushes to use the wibbly-wobbly web to get customers.

Yet to create the biggest opportunities, in terms of reaching the key customers who could bring a real change for your business while using the least amount of money to get right under their little noses – I mean the noses of the decision makers – then this old-fashioned traditionalist would always choose direct mail to make biggest impact.

I have sent handwritten letters, parcels and teddy bears and even delivered a life-size moving dragon to get myself noticed by the right people.

Pete Howard is a client of mine and a fantastic business owner who's a real master of lumpy mail – stuff, rather than words. His company does same-day deliveries in Cambridge in England. He sends prospects jars of lollipops, toy helicopters and even pretend sticks of dynamite. All are unusual, all get him noticed, grabbing attention and getting leads for his business.

Handwritten letters

The handwritten letter doesn't get thrown away. It's remembered, and very often cherished. In my first book, I told the story of how Gucci sent Aaron, the MD for our companies, a thank-you note after he'd bought from them. This handwritten note had great power in taking someone from customer to advocate.

We love to send handwritten letters to customers after they've done business with us. It means a lot to them.

Free trials

Free trials, or try before you buy, often gets overlooked, but it's mega-powerful because it removes all risk for the customer.

I know it can't work for every business. You can't build a free swimming pool and say 'Here you are, but you'll have to buy the next one'. But when you can give for free, the power it has is astronomical.

Giving is the start of receiving. Try free trials - free for a month.

Sales letters

Sales letters that get put in the post with a stamp on, that look genuine and real, as if they are from a distant relative or a pen pal of years gone by, really do work. This trick is one of my favourite ways to get customers. We don't want something that shouts out 'This is advertising'. If it looks personal, you'll have a far higher chance that it will be welcomed and read.

The sales letter is the powerhouse in keeping attention and getting action after your new potential customer has ripped open the envelope in glorious anticipation of news from Aunty Pat and her adventurous tales.

How long should a sales letter be? As long as it needs to be, so long as it's good.

I personally know of someone who sends 10-page sales letters. They work – they have brought him millions of pounds' worth of sales.

A good sales letter should contain one of these three elements: it should be *entertaining, educational* and *emotional.* Preferably it should be all three.

It should be entertaining to read so they keep reading; educational so they learn something from our expertise, and emotional by playing on the pain points for your readers to relate you to their needs.

Along with these elements, we need to craft AIDA into the letter. How can we keep attention, how can we keep interest and get a decision to be made, and how can we create a sense of urgency to act now?

Sales letter success comes from amplifying the pain you will solve for your prospect and mapping out exactly how you will do it. You are the miracle tablet that cures their migraine.

Let's take a fictional leisure attraction and a letter to sell memberships:

Dear Customer

Membership Now Available

Instead of paying each time you visit AB Farm, a membership means that you come to us as often as you like.

You can buy your membership for £65 at our admissions area when you next come in. You will need to fill in a form and then we will take payment.

We have a lot of things going on that you can come to as a member, but don't forget your membership cards or you won't be able to come in.

If you have any questions you can come and see us on

site or you can call us between 10am and 11am or 2pm and 3pm on Tuesdays and Thursdays.

Yours faithfully

Mr B Smith
Membership Advisor

Or let's take everything we've learnt and send a letter like this:

Hello James

<u>Would you like unlimited visits to Marsh Farm for a few pence a day?</u>

If you'd like to visit Marsh Farm whenever you want, make sure you read this letter right to the end.

We've been speaking to lovely customers, just like you, who've visited us and told us **they'd like to visit more often, but are limited by their family budget.**

So we took this on board and with our NEW membership, <u>you can enjoy unlimited visits to Marsh Farm for just 18p a day.</u>

Here's How It Works...

From the comfort of your armchair, visit our website and click on the membership link (you'll find it at www.marshfarm.co.uk/membership). Complete the simple membership/Direct Debit form and we'll be ready to welcome you as a member when you next visit with your membership card ready to pick up.

It really is that simple.

Laughter, family memories and acres of fun guaranteed!

As a member you can visit all our events throughout the year **WITHOUT ANY ADDITIONAL COSTS.** You'll always have somewhere to bring the kids and we've special member events and offers that we'll surprise you with too!

Don't just take our word for it...

Here's what Lisa S, a new member told us" *My family love Marsh Farm but visiting more often was just beyond our budget. But your membership has made is so affordable. The kids are always so excited to come, whether for a few hours or full day, and there's something new to see and do throughout the year. It's easy to set up, paying monthly spreads the cost and I love the special member events. Thank you Marsh Farm - y**ou've made my family very happy.**"*

Don't Miss Out
You can visit Marsh Farm from tomorrow by completing your online membership now. If you have queries then call us on 01245 321552, we're here to help.

We look forward to seeing you at Marsh Farm very soon.

Lisa Smith
Marsh Farm, Memberships

PS The online application is so easy, you can spread the cost with monthly payments and visit us as a member from TOMORROW!

Speaking in public

Speaking on stage is a powerful and super-valuable skill. I understand that for some it is more terrifying than their worst nightmare, while others, like me, just naturally love it. There are so many ways we can improve our performance and get better.

When you get up 'on stage', the idea should be that you present the best version of you – not someone else you're pretending to be for the occasion. So many people, when they get up to speak, morph into someone strangely different – they seize up and talk like robots, take recourse to pompous, long-winded language or try to pretend to be an entertainer, like they've seen on the telly. It's embarrassing, and it never works. You MUST be yourself, but be **the best version of you there is**. The good news is that with experience, most people find they lose the fear, find their own style and develop into good public speakers – it's all about practice, preparation and really knowing your stuff.

Even for those of us who are fortunate enough to be confident in front of an audience, there's a lot to learn about structure, content and how to keep people's attention.

I have found that speaking at conferences is still my biggest lead source for the best quality leads. Trust me, it's worth it. Here's something you can do from speaking, collect data and make friends with it. I do this by saying, 'If you've loved what I have done today, leave me your business card at the end and I'll send you a free copy of my book'. This works beautifully for small audiences as it promotes a conversation at the end. For bigger audiences I do the same, but say 'Text this number and I'll send you my book. When they text, you collect their details.

Next time you can actually sell from the stage, deliver a wow presentation on all the problems you solve, then make a unique offer to those who sign up on the day. There's a lot more to this if you want to master the art. I have spent hours, read tons and studied the best who deliver this. This chapter is a whistle stop tour of the art. If it's whetted your appetite, you can learn lots from my videos on speaking at jamessinclair.net.

Seminars, free and paid for

Depending on your sector and whether your ACV (average customer value) is decent, it's worth putting on a discovery day or seminar offering great advice and information around your product or service. This method is really good for converting prospects to customers and meeting many prospects at once rather than one to one. It's a time saver and informative to the customer.

This method has made us million of pounds of sales and created many advocates really quickly. Prospects who have never met us have been to one of my seminars and become clients after four hours. Admittedly some of them have read my books or seen my video content, but still this is part of our journey.

Seminars and discovery days work. Make them great, show how good you are and enjoy the process. It's a good way to get either cold or warm leads over the line.

Webinars

Webinars are of course seminars conducted on the web. There are plenty of free platforms that'll let you host a webinar. They are a good way to reach a lot of people compared to a live seminar, but they'll never have the same impact, in my opinion. Still, they have worked for us and got us customers, so they get a place in my list.

Most people try and sell something on a webinar at the end, which at the very least should be an offer with a call to action to act now.

A couple of things to be aware of: lots of viewers don't stay till the end, and conversion is only around 5%. To catapult that figure, offer a free consultation call at the end of the webinar – this will quadruple conversions. Again make sure this is not just offered at the end but referred to throughout. I know of some who have hit a better than 50% conversion rate using this method.

Video marketing card

I have discovered these little fellas to be super powerful. They're like sending a cheap iPad in the post, built into a printed book. Think of it like a birthday card that you open to find a video inside – an actual video of you talking to your customer.

If there's a tiny juggernaut out there that can deliver you a truckload of business, then this could really work for you. Send your video pad in the post as a book and make it as personal as possible, so that the prospect really takes notice.

If you want to get under the nose of someone who can really grow your business, then use this – it has worked for us. It'll cost at the time of writing around £40 to get one of these, and there are plenty of people that do them – a quick Google will find you someone.

Use names

Names are one of the most powerful tools we can use in marketing, even more powerful than the word YOU. If someone of importance, for the right reasons, remembers or uses your name, you get that little buzz inside, a feeling of achievement because someone knows your name who you thought wouldn't.

Whenever you can use the name of your prospects, it'll turbo-charge the chance that they'll come to you as a customer.

Personalising letters, emails and videos lights a fire under their effectiveness. When you look at the gifting market, online personalisation is the winner.

Give gift bags

In our nurseries, after showing round potential new clients or meeting a high-ACV prospect, we like to send a gift bag or a gift just to show we haven't forgotten them and that we really appreciate their time with us.

This works – it's a proven fact. So why do so many not do it? Do you?

Answer the phone!

Answering the phone, or NOT answering it, I am sure is the way in which businesses lose most opportunities. Everyone in your organisation should have a culture which ensures that if the phone rings, we answer happily and confidently ready to serve. I mean everyone.

Encourage check-ins

PR from your customers has never been so easy now we have social media. If someone checks in to your business and it's a physical location, imagine this: they'll let everyone know on their social following that they're doing business with you.

We humans have a sheep mentality. When buying from companies, we like to place our money where the other significant people in our lives place their pennies.

We need to encourage this. To create easy wins for this to happen, we ask our teams to ask our customers to check in – and guess what, people do!

Tap into communities and tribes

Nestle in and add value to tribes and communities. If I wanted to sell tents, I'd find Facebook groups or newsletter with lots of cub and scout leaders and make friends in those micro tribes.

With the head of the community's permission, add in video value and competitions to enhance the tribe's position. This could be the best way we've gotten to a group. It has the biggest depth and active online and offline communities. Whether it's Facebook groups or the Women's Institute, it has been my go-to place for marketing our services

Surveys

The internet is littered with free survey platforms offering up to a certain number of contacts. We use Survey Monkey as our preferred option. Sending surveys to people who have done business with you is a great way to follow up by finding out what else you can do for them and how much they love you.

Pixels and cookies for re-marketing

This book isn't a technical bible, so take what you will and please investigate further. You can add a pixel from Facebook on your website and then follow people around on the other platforms like YouTube or internet search engines and social pages to re-market. Lots of people start as browsers and need to see you a few times to get over the line. For the most part this is free to do until they click on your re-marketing ads.

Follow up

Following up is where too many businesses fail, so make sure you create a system to do it. Technology through a CRM is a great way to systematise this, because *never forget, people forget*.

Demand follow up.
Demand it by all means necessary.
Follow up in person.
Follow up by phone.
Follow up by text.
Follow up by email.

Note – most people follow up with an email, which is fine - *if* you want mediocre results. Put the effort into it. Those that show up win the day.

Chapter 7

Writing to get customers

In our quest to get customers, we will need to put a lot of time into finding the right words. The words we use and the way they are arranged will make all the difference – like a plane taking off or staying firmly parked at the airport.

You have to get good at writing copy. At the very minimum, you need to know what good copy looks like (and sounds like, in the mind of the customer reading it). Whether it's an email, leaflet, website or brochure, copy is key, together with layout, design and images.

Let's walk through the structure of copy-based marketing and then finish this little chapter with examples of it in action. When you understand this, every time a piece of marketing is presented to you, you'll be able to review it and go 'wahoo!' or 'boohoo!' immediately.

As I made clear earlier, I care more about the heading than anything else. A powerful heading grabs attention. I have spent my career testing headings, asking for opinions, brainstorming the ideas with our team to decide which is going to work best.

It goes further. We have tested different headings, especially on emails, to see which gets the highest opening rates with the same content, so we know it's the heading that's making the difference. Mailshot specialists such as the big insurance companies are past masters of this art – they'll send out 100,000 mailshots in three different versions and then measure the response to each. Operating like this soon teaches you what works and what doesn't.

The skill of the copywriter

We can all write reasonable English, I hope. So we should all be able to write our own copy, right?

Wrong. Being able to write down information and being able to write to SELL are two completely different things. Most of us learn to write to put facts across, to keep a record, or sometimes to entertain people, to tell stories or to make them laugh. Copywriting in marketing isn't about that (with exceptions I'll come to later) – it is all about getting people to buy.

The art of the copywriter is to use words to reach inside the mind of the reader and press the secret buttons that make them want to do something. Specifically, to make them want to buy your product.

Ask most non-marketeers to write some copy about their company's product or service and you'll get a description of it – a long and boring one. How big it is, what it weighs, what it's made of, how fast it goes round, how it was designed, how many different models there are, what they all cost. If you want people to buy it, this won't do. That's a fact sheet, not a sales message.

The first requirement is to get back to those all-important three Ms – Market, Message and Media.

94

Market, Message, Media

Market

Who is your customer? Are you selling to old people or young? Are they wealthy or poor? Do they live in high-rise flats or detached houses, in Harrow or in Halifax? Are they parents? Grandparents? Single and free? Children? Staid and conventional, or adventurous free spirits? What do they love – music, motorcycles or mountains? Fine wine, football or fashion? Are they ordinary people who like things put plainly and simply, or clever types who will be irritated and patronised by what they see as 'dumbed-down' language?

Now what about the competition – why are people buying rival products and not yours? What do they like about competitors' products, and what do they not like? What do they say about yours, if they use it?

And very important – **do they know you**? Are you talking to people who are already customers, or people who have never heard of you – or somewhere in between? Until you have answered these questions, you won't be able to get your message right.

The first thing you notice about copywriters – at least, the good ones – is that they don't give you the answers until they've asked some questions – a lot of questions. They will ask all the questions above, and more. They will ask all about the product or service, what it does, what it doesn't do, what it's made of, what its name is and why, what its rivals do and don't do, what market research has revealed, and so on. That's because if they are really going to nail a product, get to its soul, really understand why people love it or should love it, they need to know EVERYTHING about it. Even if the final copy is only going to be 50 words. Even if it's only a headline. Because they need to be the RIGHT words, the ones that will press the button to make the customer buy (or subscribe, or join, or whatever it is you want them to do, in those crucial few seconds when you have their attention).

If you keep proper tabs on your customers, you or your colleagues should have these answers already. Yet pro copywriters are often dismayed to find their client can't answer their questions, at least, not all of them, and not accurately. If you don't know why people buy or don't buy your product, how can your copywriter know which buttons to press? A copywriter I know once took a brief to write some promotional material about a new range of office printers. The client told him they were the fastest machines on the market, so he produced some great copy all about speed. Only after the material had been printed did he find out that it wasn't true – the new range was actually pretty average on speed. The client hadn't looked at the competition properly.

If you don't know the answers, or if you're in a start-up or new product/market situation, you need to find out. This is a job for market research, conducted either internally or by an outside company. If you've decided to get into the lawnmower market, find out all about people's attitudes to lawnmowers – what they need from them, what they are not getting right now. Maybe people are looking for cheaper lawnmowers, or lighter ones, or quieter ones, or mowers that are small enough for tiny lawns, or cute and pretty ones, or super-reliable ones, or ones that drive themselves and then take the cuttings to the tip. Find out.

Of course, the product you're making should have been designed with the benefit of market research to meet an identified need or desire. If it hasn't, the finest copy in the world won't save you – but that's a topic for another book.

Message

So now you know who you're talking to, what are you going to say to them? What need or desire are you going to address? And critically, what exactly do you want your customer to do when they have read your words – is it to place an order, sign up for a loyalty scheme, subscribe to a newsletter, come to an event, or what? It will nearly always be just ONE of those things. If you try to persuade the reader to do several things, as we said above when we talked about throwing one ball at a time, your message will lack focus and they probably won't do any of them. Not only that, you need to TELL the reader exactly what you want them to do – 'click here to save 50%', or 'beat the deadline and sign up for FREE membership here today'.

Media

How are you going to get your message through to your punters? What newspapers or magazines do they read? What social media do they follow? What TV or radio channels do they follow? Where are they likely to see posters, or pick up flyers?

Now that you know the person you're addressing, you can work out which media will reach them. No point in placing an ad for fast food in a health magazine, or distributing a flyer for high-end kitchens around a council estate. And you won't make a lot of money by advertising a service nationally when it's only available in east Surbiton.

Slogans that stick

Here are some advertising slogans which all nailed it for the product – just a few words, but they all made millions for their companies:

Kills germs dead (Domestos)
That's why mums go to Iceland (Iceland)
Because I'm worth it (L'Oreal)
We try harder (Avis)
It does exactly what it says on the tin (Ronseal)

If you think those slogans were just tossed out by a bunch of smarty-pants executives sitting round a table pulling ideas out of the air, think again. They represent the tip of a huge iceberg of research and understanding into what's at the heart of these products and services – what really is the key reason for people to identify with it, love it and buy into it.

That's why the same principle applies to all commercial copywriting – you need to do your homework before you put a word down on paper. You need to know where those secret buttons are and how to press them. Sometimes getting it right is a long learning process – not just for the copywriter but for the company itself, and it's intimately involved with fundamentals of marketing. But it's worth it, like L'Oreal.

Overcoming resistance

The most painful part of writing copy is that most people will never read it. A tragic fact, but true. It's easy to imagine all those thousands of eager punters ripping open your mailshot or clicking on the links on a website – but that ain't the real world. In the real world, most people won't take a blind bit of notice of your carefully chosen, painstakingly researched words.

Your job is to find out WHY. There won't be one reason – there will probably be several, maybe lots. To deal with them, you need to look on the dark side. You need to dream up all the reasons why someone WOULDN'T want to read your copy. Draw up a list of 'why wouldn't they' and then shoot them all down in your copy.

Here's an example a list of the reasons why a customer wouldn't buy mail order steak:

I'm not going to buy because...

– I don't believe these steaks are going to be as good as they say.
– I don't think people really buy meat by mail order.
– It's probably going to cost a fortune to phone you up and place my order.

98

- I don't want to phone up, I don't like talking to people.
- You probably won't accept my credit card, and that'd be super awkward.
- I haven't got a stamp.
- I think the steak will arrive spoiled.
- I might not like the look of the meat when it arrives.
- I don't know how to cook steak.

Every single one of those objections can be dealt with and demolished in the letter (it would be a longish letter, but as I said earlier, long copy can work really well once you've aroused the prospect's Interest along your path through AIDA).

Writing for two kinds of readers at once

People read in different ways – there are those who read through copy word for word and those that skim. Sometimes they can be the same person at different points on the AIDA journey. The skimmers are just clocking the headings, bullet points, chapter headings, words emphasized in bold or italics, quotes and diagrams. The actual body text is the last thing they read, and they will never read it at all if the other stuff doesn't get their interest. Most people skim read, because they can't afford to waste time and will only read the full copy if what they've skimmed first has grabbed their attention

When you understand that people will read your marketing message in different ways, you will understand why your copy must follow a **dual readership path** – one route for the word-by-word reader, the plodder who will read most of what you write (this guy's in the minority), and one for the skimmer, who will breeze over your copy, stopping to read only what grabs his attention.

As pros at getting customers, we will always write for both the skimmer and the plodder using the dual readership path. As readers we are time poor, and we only want to go where our time is best used. People don't read every word unless they are motivated to do so by the copy you've carefully chosen and how you've chosen to *cosmetically* enhance it.

What's perhaps even more important (especially if you think you think you know how to navigate the dual readership path, but you're actually making the same mistake as everyone else), is that skimmers do not read words or phrases that *look* the same as all the other words or phrases on the page.

In other words, if you cosmetically enhance important stuff to make it stand out, you can't do the same with non-essential copy right next to it or the skimmer will skip all of it. You can't emphasise everything. So use bold type, italics and capitals sparingly. If everything is bold, nothing stands out. And if you put whole sentences in capitals, readers will feel you are shouting at them. It's also been proved that it's harder to read words in capitals.

On the Net of course, it's easy to put all the small stuff on a separate page, so it doesn't get in the way – it's just there if it's needed, usually by the serious buyer who wants to check the small print or the technical details before pressing the 'buy now' button.

Knowing your copy will be skimmed – and it will be – means we can plan for that.

Skimmers focus on:

- Capitalisation – but remember capitals are harder to read and can look like shouting, so they should be used sparingly, just a word or two at a time.

- Bold type – with the same proviso as for capitals.

- Underlining – strictly on one word or phrase at a time, if you must use it, or you'll look like a crazy person.

- Text that's in a different colour from the rest – but be aware that it will add to the print cost and it won't work on photocopies.

- Bigger type.
- Italics.
- Bulleted lists.
- Numbered Lists.
- Boxes, circles or cut-out lines.
- Shading/background colour.
- Changes in font (but very sparingly).

Exclamation marks are great for drawing attention to the importance of short key statements, like 'It's free!' Or 'Do it today!' But just like all the other emphasis techniques, never overuse them, or their effect will be lost.

What's the best way to make every line of your copy get read? Use a bulleted list. Because:

■ People see bulleted items as more important.

■ They find bulleted lists easier to follow.

■ They are more likely to read every word.

■ If they're skimming, they'll find it easier to spot the features they are looking for.

None of the above techniques for punching prospects in the eye should be used to excess, or it will look as if you're shouting, and customers do not like being shouted at any more than you do.

Remember that your copy as a whole needs to hang together to make sense to the reader who ONLY notices the bulleted lists, the capitals, the words in bold and those which are underlined.

Customer first, product last

Most great sales copy is written backwards, from the point of view of the customer's desires, frustrations, wants, thoughts and feelings and the pain the company can take away. By contrast, most ineffective copy starts with the company, its features and benefits, its superiority in the marketplace and its price differential, and by the time it tells you why you should buy, zzzzz, you've gone to sleep.

The deadly headline

The heading grabs attention, so as I said earlier, it has to be right for your target audience. Get the heading wrong and you can kiss goodbye to your investment.

Headlines are critical. It's said that five times as many people read the headline as the body copy, so you'd better make sure yours is a good one. The purpose of the headline is not to boast about your product – it's to get the punter to read what follows.

Here are the kinds of headlines that work best:

'How To' headlines:
How to start losing weight today

How to shrink your waist in just 4 minutes a day

'Secret' Headlines
A secret-led headline can really capture the attention of your reader:

The 6 secrets that will fix your copywriting confusion

The secret that dentists don't want you to know about naturally white teeth

Use numbers

Using numbers is a key way to get people reading – but remember to pick numbers that sound precise, not round numbers which sound like vague estimates:

13 steps towards great copywriting

37 ways to make the most of your lunch

7 simple principles to keep wrinkles at bay

Our research shows '7' is the best number to use. My super-dooper friend Mark Creaser, the best copywriter I know, came up with this next line, and it's a corker. It attracted so many leads to his marketing business:

Here's why you'll benefit massively from investing in property, without using any of your own money.

Other examples of 'How I', 'Here's how' and 'Here's why' headlines:

Here's how to pay off your mortgage in 7 years
How I overcame joint pain and got back in the game.
How I added 20 yards to my golf drives

Guarantee headlines

Offering to remove the risk can be a really effective way to engage with your reader.

Sell your home in 7 days or less – guaranteed
Pizza ordered and delivered in 25 minutes or your next order FREE!

'DON'T' is a powerful word to get people in – it's a hook we've dangled many times. It startles the reader, because it is telling them NOT to something. Huh? They read on...

Don't invest in property this year until you've read this.
Don't buy a coolbox. Buy a plug-in fridge.

NOW...
'Now' is a great word to kick off a heading with. I like this one:

Now is not the time to get a job. It's the time to start a business.

NEW!
NEW has been one of the most powerful words in advertising since... well, since advertising was invented. It's the quickest attention-grabber we use in our leisure marketing: NEW management, NEW for 2020, NEW restaurant open Friday.

List your ideas, then pick the best

Don't stop as soon as you come up with what looks like a good headline, because the first headline that you write is unlikely to be the best one. Write out 10 or more, until you find a combination of words that is more powerful and more compelling than any of the others.

Tell them a story

We all love stories. We NEED stories. We make sense of the world through them, right from the cradle. Start telling a story, and if you do your job right, the reader will stick with you through pages of copy.

BUT – your story must be:

- Relevant – make sure the people and the setting are ones that are familiar to your reader.
- Interesting – make sure the story has a beginning, a middle and an ending that has an element of surprise.
- Simple – no boring detail or waffle.

Credibility

When you make claims in your copy, they must be credible, and you must be able to back them up. This means they should be **precise** – If your investors are seeing an average return of 21.2 per cent a year, give that figure, not 'over 20%'. Otherwise it will sound like a guesstimate, or a vague boast.

The best way to convince your punters that you're telling the truth is to use **testimonials**, as referred to earlier. Social media give us lots of new ways of garnering testimonials. But they must have a name beside them.

With some products and services, particularly the more technical and complex ones, a **case study** works well – a detailed account of how the product or service sorted out a problem or improved results. B2B marketeers rely heavily on case studies.

Use the right voice

I mentioned earlier how some people can turn a golden public-speaking opportunity into a toe-curling failure by adopting a fake personality. The same thing applies to writing sales copy. So many writers who don't have a professional copywriting background undergo a change in personality when they try to write sales copy – they go all dry and technical, or too jokey, or lofty, or pompous.

Imagine you've just come back from giving a technical presentation to a formal industry gathering about how a new photo imaging system works on a camera. You'd prepare properly, with visuals and graphics and charts. Then when you get home, your neighbour Jim asks you about your day. You'd throw out all the formal structure and the technical detail and just say something like: 'Our new Whizzo-Snap is brilliant, it saves all the images and then just keeps the ones you want, and if you delete something by mistake you can just press a button and get it back. It's dead easy, miles better than the old way'. Friendly, simple and to the point. That's how good sales copy should read.

Proprietary language

Proprietary language, or insiders' jargon, is the use of certain phrases and words that only those in a certain community, tribe, professional world or hobbyist clique will understand. It makes its users feel they belong, while the rest of us don't. Doctors use it, lawyers use it, the police use it, and so do engineers, scientists, economists, birdwatchers, bikers and so on. Doctors and other regulated professions will use jargon or proprietary language to lure a fellow contributor to a convention.

Using proprietary language is a badge of belonging. It can add huge power when trying to build rapport with customers and new colleagues, quickly. Knowing this is especially powerful in a niche marketing space. It can show your expertise for the space and create for the prospect a feeling of 'one of us'.

In marketing it's both delicious and dangerous at the same time, because it can attract or repel a prospect. The danger lies in using it with the wrong prospect, someone who doesn't understand it, because you will immediately exclude them.

If I am doing a talk at a conference and I know the sector, I'll throw in all the proprietary language I can muster up, as it brings the audience close to me. If I'm speaking in a geographical area I know, I'll dive in to all the local in-jokes I know. Using proprietary language in niche marketing gains you trust.

If I was writing to sell something to accountants, I'd use just enough proprietary language so they know I'm in on the act – so to speak.

Be very wary of getting out of your depth with proprietary language. If you strike a false note by using a word or phrase wrongly, you will be exposed as a phoney, which could turn your ad – and you – into a laughing stock. Ideally, make sure the words are written by someone who is already an insider – If you're marketing holidays in Scotland, hire a copywriter who's lived north of the border, or if it's to promote a golf course, get a writer who plays golf. One travel brochure copywriter wrote about Scottish people playing the claymore, believing it was a traditional musical instrument – oops, no it's a sword. The client laughed his socks off. Right before he sacked the copywriter.

Selling on emotion

People don't act rationally – not even people acting for their businesses. If they did, they would buy on logic, like robots. They buy things because they want them, not because they need them. They buy for emotional reasons – so in writing sales copy, you need to understand which emotion to harness.

Everyone shares the same emotional needs. Everyone wants, to varying degrees, to:

- Be wealthy.
- Be healthy.
- Be popular.
- Be secure.
- Be attractive.
- Be free to do what they want.
- Have fun.
- Find inner peace.

Successful products and brands all promise to satisfy one or more of these emotions. A new sports bike will make you feel healthy and free, a Volvo will make you feel secure, a Porsche will help you to have fun (and feel wealthy and attractive), a Jeep will give you freedom – and maybe giving up your car and investing in a season ticket on public transport will make you wealthy, healthy and find inner peace. So it goes on. This is why your copy needs to make people appreciate how your product or service will satisfy one of these key needs. They have to *feel* it.

Using design to make your words hit home

Big companies invest in design to build brands that customers instantly recognize, so they'll repurchase. But that doesn't mean design comes first. The design serves the message, not the other way round. Design should be used to make the most of the headline, the copy and the call to action, in order to get customers.

I'm presuming you're not Coca Cola here, so let's look at design with copy.

- It should catch the eye – know how to make it stand out and grab attention.
- Make it relevant to the target audience. What is their design anchor? To understand this, look at the design of the magazines they read, the shops they shop in and the coffee shops they frequent.
- If it looks busy and complicated, it is, and you're going to lose potential customers.
- White space is allowed, and should be embraced. It helps the eye to focus on the words, the bit that matters.
- Whether you personally like it or not is irrelevant, because you probably aren't the target audience. Does reading your marketing piece make the customers feel like they belong? That's the aim of the design.

No one cares about your logo

You're the only person who cares about your logo, so don't let it take ownership of your headline message and call to action. It's folly to let it take more of your marketing space than anything else, yet unpractised marketeers still do this. Sometimes a bossy CEO or chair who doesn't have a marketing background will instruct the team to make the logo bigger or bolder. You need to tell them why that's a bad move. The logo, corporate colours etc are just there as part of the branding, to remind the buyer who they're buying from. It's a familiar face, like a car badge or a brand name on a camera or TV set. They are never the main message. The values of the brand are more important than the look of the logo.

The vital call to action

NEVER forget the lessons of Chapter 4. Your call to action needs to be clear, firm and direct, eg:

– Contact us by September 30 to take advantage of this unrepeatable offer.
– Sign and mail your form TODAY for a lifetime of peace of mind.
– Call [number] to order NOW.

To sum up:

– Know who you customer is.
– Start with Market, Message, Media.
– Sell the way your product is going to make customers feel, not what it does.
– Shoot down all the reasons NOT to buy.
– Make your copy clear and direct.
– Develop a great headline that makes people read the rest.
– Tell stories.

- Use testimonials.
- Sell to people's emotional needs.
- Finish with a bang – the all-important call to action.

Chapter 8
Final thoughts

You need to become much more to your customer than just the product or service you supply. Get them emotionally involved. We're selling to the heart, then the head, and we need them to believe in that.

Deep down we're all softies. We need to be in business for more than just the products and services we sell.

Our teams and customers need to believe in our values and culture and get behind our vision. I love the fact that as an organisation we have our own charity and that our teams are its ambassadors, making the magic of the wishes we grant come true and raising money for the charity through our businesses' activities.

I love that our team can change people's lives through our business training and give people magical memories from coming to our events and leisure attractions. I'm passionate that our childcare business sets children up for their first steps in life and that our team knows this responsibility is bigger than the business.

Being a mover and shaker and having a real purpose means people can really get behind what you do. What's your purpose? Can people get behind it? Make sure you tell people about it with passion.

Marketeers ruin everything

Understanding this is understanding an audience's frustration. The more eyeballs something gets, the more marketeers want to market on it, and this is when we as viewers, listeners, readers and users get frustrated. Marketing and advertising ruin what we love by constantly disturbing us, stealing time away from us. The trick is to be an early adopter of the constant new platforms by taking advantage of them before the marketeers ruin them.

When commercial radio came in in the 1970s, it was rudely interrupted by adverts and more adverts, until we would all rather have had ad-free radio. The web has become a huge banner for multiple ads and clicks, until punters are desperate to get rid of the parasites we know as advertisements.

Brilliant for us marketeers, but annoying for consumers, is the software called cookies and pixels that follow us around in their quest to steal more of our attention for sales. Of course as marketeers we want this software to follow warm leads around, but as consumers they just annoy us.

My email has been ruined by marketeers, so I pay less and less attention to email marketing. That's why we now have to work harder at getting our open rates and click throughs better.

TV is just one commercial after another. Luckily, we can now record our programmes, then watch them later and fast forward past the ads so we can watch with minimal interruption. Lots of people do this just so they can skip the commercials.

Be aware of this and pivot to improve your approach. It's why I love content marketing and why it has a far higher chance of being noticed.

My closing point is this: if your email is no longer working, read some books on email marketing and listen to some podcasts, or watch YouTube videos from the smarty pants who have found out how to make it work in today's world.

Never wish your marketing was easier. Wish you were better – and you can be better.

The answers that will enable you to improve by 10% are at our fingertips – go find them. I find books amazing and this website called Google a real winner.

What you should avoid

As we approach the final pages, I thought I'd share some of my big no-nos when it comes down to the art of getting customers.

Relying solely on on-line methods is just silly. The world is a big place and so many marketeers are doing lazy, easy, on-line marketing rather than actually thinking – 'how can I get customers in the real, off-line world?' My advice is to use both. Think how you can drive people online using offline methods.

Take away the friction

Removing friction makes it easy for people to do business with you. What's friction? It's all the things that make it harder for customers to do business with you – warnings, small print, telling people what your service or product WON'T do, waffling on about waiting lists and get-out clauses, just in case they are disappointed. You do need to make it clear in the small print just what they are buying and what they are not buying and on what terms, but there's no place for this in your marketing.

If it's your business, if you're the employee of an organisation or in leadership or management, you'll become protective, like a policeman upholding the law. You'll be tempted to protect the baby you've built, to avoid any risks, to head off complaints before they happen. In doing this you'll add friction, which will make it harder for people to do business with your company. It'll get worse – you'll also be surrounding yourself with a team that will put protection methods in place.

My argument is that we've all been done over in life, if you really think about it, but that occasional joust with a nasty wotsit should be set aside when you make decisions about running a company that wants to get customers. The more little barriers you put up, the more work your prospects have to do before they can do business with you. At some point enough is enough, and they'll tire of the rules and walk away.

Amazon are great at removing friction. They allow you to buy so easily, even when it comes to books – here, have the first one free, see if you like it. So many companies would say, buy some books first, then you can have one free. My view is that giving is the start of receiving.

And don't force people into complicated contracts. Let them be free to go when they want to. If you look after them, they'll stay. For every person you create in the la la land of fantasy who is *potentially* going to do you over, remember that there are 20 who are not. Have faith that most people are not crooks. For the most part, people are decent and straight dealing.

Rules, terms, conditions and contracts scare shoppers off, let alone prospects. The job of the master customer-getter is to grease the wheels, provide the lubricant to make doing business with you easy and agreeable.

Here's a little story from our business. I'm a big fan of membership businesses, as you now know from reading this book. I have been on a long quest to turn our companies into a membership business, bringing together this philosophy with a powerful subscription business where people pay you a little bit of money a lot of the time. For the purpose of this story, I know monthly revenues kill the stress in a business. When revenue is predictable, planning becomes a whole heap easier. The hold-up for this is implementation, as with so many things in the modern world. The challenge is getting the technology to enable you to catch up with the idea.

We created the membership business we desired after we eventually got our tech to catch up. Monthly memberships grew at our venues and we wanted people to join up and stay. It's still running today and is incredibly good value, so customers are joining us. In short our members pay a low amount per month for unlimited entry. I, being the typical entrepreneur, wanted them to grow faster, and so did my team.

The friction in growth, as with many companies, was put in place by us, as in our quest for protecting the business we wanted to make sure people didn't just sign up for one month and pay the hugely discounted price instead of the normal entrance price. I was desperate to release people from friction. I wanted to just let them come and go as they please. I felt that if we did a good job, people would stay. I think if we had put less friction in place we'd have even more members in place.

I get that it's a balance. Care and thought must go in to protecting the company – to what point is the question you should be wrestling with.

My point is this: people will do you over regardless of protection. Make access to your business easy, then look after people and they'll stay.

If you can't track it, sack it

When you're growing a business from scratch, you'll know it's a quest to save cash and survive. Realising that for most the odds are against us, I have methods to start stacking the odds more evenly.

The question we purse-string holders always have to be asking is this: 'What marketing works?' This will give you a healthy fear of spending. The same applies to big companies – you should always aim to upscale your returns. Too many business people who hold the purse strings have a buyer's mentality rather than an investor's mentality when it comes to marketing.

The same rule applies no matter your size, big small or somewhere in between. If you can't track it, don't spend it.

The spend on marketing must be part of a return on investment calculator. The simplest ROI calculator is positive cash flow in divided by cash investment in, times 100 – that's your ROI as a percentage.

I like to include labour in my cash investment too. If you've spent £100,000 in labour costs on a campaign that needs to be included, not just your spend on advertising or materials.

GP Cash Flow

÷100 = ROI

Capital + Labour

Your master marketing team

Or as we should call it: 'the Getting Customers team'

I said earlier in this book that you need to be the ringleader with an outline understanding of all aspects of business, never one of the acts in the circus - a specialist in one particular aspect. This will allow you to ask all the right questions when talking to the boffins who do have that specialist knowledge – you'll need to know enough to sniff out the bull.

Taking that principle, here are some of my thoughts on the 'wizards' or star performers I think you'll need when assembling your marking team.

When it comes to running our companies, my default position is this – I'm naturally an in-house guy. I like my team near me and around me to get it all done. However we still solicit the help of others when we need the latest on-point advice – usually digital. When looking to use an outside company, look for individual specialists who can help you. In the marketing world it seems that so many are jacks of all trades and masters of none. In many cases that's too much like you, and you don't want to employ another you. When it comes to expert advice, we need experts, specialists.

Beware of the marketing agency rookie who is looking to extract pounds from your business for services under the claim, 'I do PPC, build websites, design materials, edit and write copy'. They can only be average at each task. The best person I have met who does FB ads ONLY does FB ads.

Highly effective and successful people have a common trait. They know what they want to build before they start – they think with the end in mind. This gives them a distinct advantage when it comes to success.

Here's the team I have assembled as my go-to pros – what might be your future dream team, my little army of getting-customer warriors. I'm not telling you that you need them all now, but the cold hard fact is this: if you want to crack the code of getting customers on a humungous scale, then you'll need a team like this. You just can't do everything yourself.

I started with one person when I got going, but I always planned that in the years to come I would have a team of talented superstars to help. Stage 1 of building a team is to think what your team will look like from the get-go. This will help you find them when the time comes.

You and I are never going to stop recruiting talented people. If they're good they'll be profitable for you straight away. My nose is always on the hunt for talent. I recruit good people and ask them to write their own job description for what they can do for our company – no joke.

My view is this and always has been. Average people want to work for average people, good people want to work for good people and excellent people... well, you get the idea.

The better you are the better you become, and the better the people out there will be attracted to you.

When you assemble a team, never start with money. Start with the vision of where the company is going. When you've agreed the right package, always remember this.

If you want to motivate your people, educate them. This will trump the short-term endorphin rush from a pay rise or a bonus. When people are learning and growing, they're motivated beyond belief.

Your team of professors

The brain

The brain is in many cases YOU, because you're going to be the objective setter who sets out what's going to happen. A well-written brief and a documented plan on paper provide the set of instructions which will drive the success of each campaign you carry out.

The scribe

The ability to write well is critical when it comes to marketing, as explained in the last chapter, and I am in awe of amazing copywriters. The simple fact is that great copy can hugely increase your results. The words you use can be the difference between success and failure. Please don't be shy to pay some pennies to a great copywriter who knows their craft.

For success, you need to be able to understand what good copy is when it's presented to you.

The designer who gets the brand

You'll need your designer to follow the brand guidelines of your business, so if you haven't created such a thing, you should. This investment in creating a set of brand guidelines, documented of course, saves time, money and energy and will leave you with a far happier result from your marketing efforts.

We create these for all our brands, stating what colours, fonts and types of language and image can be used. The brief saves time, but also gets what design can do, to control the eye to take the actions we want the potential customer or existing customer to take.

The photo whizz

People seriously underestimate the importance of good images – a great photo can sell so much more than a poor one. You'll need to have someone who can produce images of your products that literally make people want to buy. Food photography is a good example of visual genius at work. In our business people are at the centre, so the chances are that your most valuable images will be great pictures of your customers. People pictures are a different skill from food photography or technical work, so you may need different photographers for different assignments. No photographer is great at everything.

The edit is as important as the take. Take some time to really perfect your shoots and you'll see many more clickthroughs online and more action takers offline.

We tested this with our products in our make-a-bear company. When we sent well-edited photos to our platforms of the same product our click throughs and engagement increase by 100%.

Good photography is a great investment – it's not a cost.

The Steven Spielberg

Video is now a crucial part of our marketing mix in terms of the type of content we put out, and it's growing. Great video trumps great photography.

To get great results from content marketing, you'll need someone who loves the subject you're making content about. Let me explain. If you're making content marketing about fishing, find a videographer who loves fishing. This has been my secret sauce for my content on entrepreneurship. My videographer and the head of the James Sinclair brand, Mike Chudley, or 'Chudders' as I affectionately call him, loves entrepreneurship and takes a genuine interest in the subject. This means he loves what he edits and gets the audiences interest – he

IS my audience. This gives us a distinct advantage. He knows what he would like to watch, so he shoots better content.

You'll want good cuts to hold the audience. I like a cut every 10 seconds – at least. You'll always have subtitles as most people watch in silence. At the time of writing over 80% of video is watched on mute!

Thumbnails (the still pic before the video starts) are essential and must contain a 'what's in it for me' heading. For example 'How to cook a brilliant steak' will start with a picture of a steak. This is different from the video heading description. Watch me and Chudders talk about our video marketing top tips by going to YouTube and typing 'Top tips for video marketing – James Sinclair'.

The adwords guru

Pay per click is a minefield because if you get it wrong, you and your pennies will disappear like you've got a hole in your pocket, and you'll have nothing to show for them.

This is an area where soliciting the help of a pro is essential. Again a base knowledge will hugely help. You need to know the right questions to ask to sniff out the real professors amongst the jacks of all trades.

PPC, on search or on social, we've participated in heavily. The success is always down to fine detail, decreasing your cost per click and reaching a bigger audience. If your margins are low or your average transaction is not frequent, it'll soon wind you up. It did me.

We spent some £300,000 marketing our party shop and we brought in £450,000 in sales. Before we go any further down this little garden path, I'd like to point out that we don't run party shops online or offline any more. Here's why.

I didn't care back in the day when I was skinny and youth was my friend that this didn't cover the cost of time and product because we had got ourselves a customer. In my youth and naivety, I thought that person would transact more with us in the future and then we'd make some money that way. Silly, silly boy! The problem with this type of business was that the customer only bought once. Our biggest selling lines were weddings and baby shower stuff. To this day, I hate losing money on sales, but then failing to get future lifetime sales was just depressing. You could argue that some of those people had more children later, or split up and got married again, but whatever the reason, they were certainly not *easy* regular sales.

The point to the story is this: PPC works. It gets you enquiries, and fast, if you have a good follow up. Just make sure you have a customer value plan which allows for the profit to come on the second or third sale, not the acquisition sale. This will give you the faith to carry on.

In terms of my tips on PPC and how to get the most out of it, it's back to AIDA again. The rule that you must grab attention, keep it and get your prospect to act applies here too, and in your PPC ads – you must fight for and win the sale. Lastly, get yourself a whizz who knows their onions on how to drive cost per clicks down and pinpoint your exact audience.

The CRM techy pro

The tech stuff we can do with CRM (customer relationship management) puts the magic into taking a customer through the journey to sales. We look for CRM stars that are proven for the industries we operate in – why be the guinea pig if you don't have to be? To be successful, model what's been done before, adapt and improve it.

For our leisure business we use Microsoft Dynamics and for our business training company we use Infusionsoft. Both are fantastic at taking enquiries and leads through a journey to sales and future sales.

As Wikipedia puts it: *'Customer relationship management is an approach to manage a company's interaction with current and potential customers. It uses data analysis about customers' history with a company to improve business relationships with customers, specifically focusing on customer retention and ultimately driving sales growth'.*

That sums these little beauties up perfectly. Luckily for us bootstrapped, penny-pinching entrepreneurs, gone are the days of super expensive investments in tech fantasy land. There are so many off-the-shelf wonders that will work for your business on a monthly rolling subscription that for the ROI can reach 1000% or more. it gets better, because they keep developing so you don't have to.

A CRM system can track how warm a customer is, how often they do business with you, if they've opened an email, called you before, and much more.

My advice is to start basic but stay consistent in your aims and efforts, then get better. Understanding the building of a CRM system will take some smart expertise. Get it right and it'll pay dividends. We have called on the help of the pros here, but again we get a base knowledge ourselves to get more out of the wizards and their long beards of wisdom.

The funnel pro

When I sit with my clients to help grow their businesses, I grab some pens and a flip chart, establish how much profit they are looking for and work out what revenue we need to bring in to get it. Then we quickly move on to our ideal customer. This then lays the foundation to building a funnel. At the bottom of our funnel we put the ideal customer, the one who makes us the most money, and at the top we put in all the trip wires which could stop them becoming followers (as mentioned above in the chapter on funnels).

The chapter above and my statement here describe how funnels work. What really gets me excited is being able to design an on-line funnel that turns prospects into customers.

Building a funnel that works can be so much better than a website or a Facebook page. The right funnel can make you some serious money, and quickly.

The granddaddy of this in marketing online is a chap from the good old USA called Russel Brunson. Companies like his will give you great ways of designing quick and easy funnels without the need of programmers or techie heads, for a monthly subscription. (No, I'm not paid to say this.)

The presenter

If you're inspired by my routes to create content marketing or podcasts to get customers that are ready to buy because they've seen your content, then you'll need to get good at presenting and keeping an audience's attention.

A good presenter will have the 4C's as described on page 13. They will have Charisma/Character, be Comfortable with being in public, know their Content inside out and be Consistent.

It doesn't have to be you who does it – it could be a team member or an influential person in your space who you sponsor. Nike did this with Michael Jordan and Tiger Woods. You could go as big as this or use an Instagram influencer who'll also share the content to their list. It's nowhere near as expensive as you might think to engage influencers who have a following – if you don't ask, you don't get. But they have to like the 'thing' and love your brand, and they need to have those 3 Cs.

The on-trend spy

The world of digital marketing is changing fast. Be aware of the new emerging platforms and get involved before the other marketeers start ruining it.

The spy will always be looking for where the eyeballs are. Is it a closed Facebook group, is it a new community group, is it a new emerging influencer? Find the eyeballs first and be present.

The content creation wizard

The secret sauce in our content marketing and in the wins we've had from it is down to Mike Chudley, or 'Chudder's as we call him. This super-talented man saw me speak, bought into our vision and has made all of my videos, creatively leading our content with me. I spend more time with Mike than anyone else. Thanks Chuds!

The secret sauce is his talent, but my biggest advice is to get a great content creator or creator team that loves the space the content is about.

I am making content on entrepreneurship; Chudders loves entrepreneurship. It's been the best move we've made. He loves the subject and directs by his opinion. This makes a huge difference.

So whatever you're making content on – get a content creator who loves it.

In Conclusion

Dear Reader

I really can't thank you enough for dedicating your time to reading my book.

I get asked on a constant basis how I get more done than most. How does anyone find the time to write books, make videos, make a daily podcast, write articles, speak here, there and everywhere and run a large company?

A couple of factors that make all this possible; you are welcome to swipe and deploy my methods.

Firstly, I shoehorn my thinking into making sure I fulfil my time with high-value tasks – like getting customers. I hate doing repeatable tasks that are unleveraged. I only want to do work that I can do once and will then continue working for ever – like writing a book, making a podcast, recording a video for my YouTube channel or buying a property or business that will generate income for years to come. This way of thinking has given me the ability to find time to focus on the ever-important task of customer acquisition, the subject of these pages which I have shared with you.

This book can help you in your quest for success, though it's a long journey of hard work and personal sacrifice. I don't want you to be under any illusion about this.

Money is the prize for sure, but progress is the beat that keeps you going. The older you get, the more knocks you get and the more experience you gather. This thing "experience" is a superb and dangerous skill we all learn. Superb because we know what works, dangerous because it can often stop us trying new things.

Secondly, you'll have gathered as you turned the pages that it's much easier to buy in the operations roles of a business, compared to the skills of getting customers for it. My experience shows that many more of us want to look after customers than actually go and get them.

I WISH I had got to grips with this essential skill far earlier on the road of entrepreneurship. It really is a skill, a talent that comes far more easily to some than others. So, please, NEVER stop learning, or you'll see your earnings deteriorate.

And never stop innovating. As I said – if you don't innovate - you'll evaporate. If your business isn't growing, it's dying.

You'll have to get to grips with the understanding that to grow a business, you'll only have a certain amount of time. To get more time you'll have to buy in other people's time. Period.

I wanted this book to take the uninitiated in the art of getting customers to the next levels, in the quest for business success. I wanted to give you gorgeous people a map which doesn't just show you where the treasure is (your customers) but gives you a step-by-step satnav on how to get to the treasure too... with warnings on how to avoid road closures, traffic jams and stormy weather. I believe that with the help of my master editors, Chris and Lyssa, I have created a treasure map that will take you to the 4 Cs.

If you break it down, nothing else really matters when it comes to business. In its simplest form, business is this... You create a product or service to the best of your abilities, that solves people's needs, then you go and get customers. Turning a profit should then be the result.

You'll remember that kid that sold sweets at school – I was that kid, I bought some product and found customers every day – profitably. The natural talent was there to harness. It's one that needs constant practice, testing and discipline, as any other skill does, to go to the next levels.

Like all good sport players that have a zest and talent for their sport, it's the coach who mentors them, who takes them from good to outstanding.

The folly of many talented "good" people, is they don't get a coach or a mentor, or read or listen to outside advice enough. You don't know it all. If you're naturally good, the right mentoring and learning can make you outstanding.

Then there are the other business owners, the people who have this talent in giant proportions, like a lion ready to roar and make the magic happen for their business. Sadly they leave it locked away in a magical wardrobe of wonder, like the one in that well-known book and film franchise. If that's you, just imagine you went back into the wardrobe and scooped your talent back up for the world to see. Who knows what wonders you'll find to make your business flourish?

My real wish, and I mean this, is that many more entrepreneurs would learn the skill and keep practising it to master the art in order to add rocket fuel to their businesses' marketing efforts.

My success in business has been down to having a slight edge on making happen things which others see as impossible, and leaving others to do the possible. I am blessed to work with a seriously amazing team that make things happen - every day. They blow me away.

Every year our team does more and grows more, to make us that little bit better. Our signature brand and group company, Partyman, is on a continued journey to build brands that families LOVE.

A company is only as good as its people... there has never been a truer saying.

To wrap up this collection of pages, I would like to pay special thanks to Aaron Othman, our MD, Janequi Carsandas, Julie Evans, Kelly Gardner, Lyssa Elster, Katie Davies, Michael 'Chudders' Chudley and Janette Stagg. Together they've worked with me in our HQ for over a century of combined service to build what we have created. Thank you so much! I love working with you through all the good times, and the few tough times too. My heart goes out to you.

Magically yours
James Sinclair

Printed in Great Britain
by Amazon

47438493R00086